T0277160

ONCE UPON *TOMORROW*

ONCE UPON *TOMORROW*

HARNESSING THE NEW OPPORTUNITIES THE METAVERSE CREATES

SHURICK AGAPITOV

Forefront
BOOKS

Published by Worth Books, an imprint of Forefront Books, Nashville, Tennessee.

Distributed by Simon & Schuster.

Library of Congress Control Number: 202392233

Print ISBN: 978-1-63763-265-9
E-book ISBN: 978-1-63763-266-6

Cover Design by Xsolla (USA), Inc.
Interior Design by Mary Susan Oleson, Blu Design Concepts

Printed in the United States of America

To builders of their own future.
To builders of the metaverse.

CONTENTS

WELCOME TO THE METAVERSE

Do you remember your excitement the very first time you used the internet?

For the first time in human history, all knowledge sits on the edge of your fingertips. Your phone, your computer, your tablet can instantly take you to any point in history, teach you complex mathematics and science, and do it all largely for free.

The internet has been the great equalizer of my lifetime. It enabled a young man in one of the poorest places in the world to educate himself and identify the possibilities that exist on every continent. As internet speeds accelerate, graphics quality improves, and more consumers migrate to the web, new opportunities will emerge.

The internet will become more powerful and immersive, and it will provide even greater opportunities for creative individuals who want to find their place in the world.

That is a major theme of this book. The chapters ahead will tell you about the next generation of the internet that I believe will advance in the next seven years: it's called the Metaverse.

Now, you might ask, "What's so important about this Metaverse?"

It's not just about 3D graphics or online speed. It is a transformational technology that will change how businesses operate, how consumers work and play, and how humans tell stories—whether for entertainment or for marketing purposes.

No longer will this world rotate around the centralized plans of big tech giants like Alphabet, Meta Platforms, or Amazon. I want to show you my vision—one that, if realized, offers you greater control of your data and privacy and gives you an incredible opportunity to create value in this work.

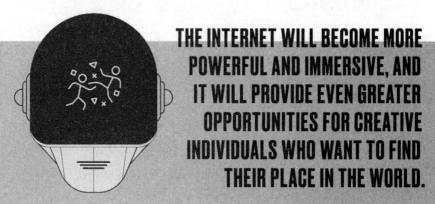

THE INTERNET WILL BECOME MORE POWERFUL AND IMMERSIVE, AND IT WILL PROVIDE EVEN GREATER OPPORTUNITIES FOR CREATIVE INDIVIDUALS WHO WANT TO FIND THEIR PLACE IN THE WORLD.

It's not just about what appears on the screen. It's not just about fancy semiconductor chips. This is a massive paradigm shift. How we interact, share stories, and create and implement ideas will be unlike anything you've experienced in your lifetime. But you need to take the time right now to learn about the future possibilities of the Metaverse and get out ahead of the pack.

This book will show you what's possible and how the Metaverse will reshape society. We'll discuss the technologies, legal challenges, and much more. We'll talk about the different approaches to how consumers will buy products and what they'll use for payments.

Let's take a journey together into the future of the Metaverse and the internet tenement.

CHAPTER 1

WHY MARK ZUCKERBERG GOT THE METAVERSE ALL WRONG

In October 2021, Facebook cofounder Mark Zuckerberg rocked the global technology industry with a shocking announcement. Seventeen years after its founding, the world's leading social networking company would radically transform.

Facebook would have a new name. A new brand. A new vision. A new "North Star," as Zuckerberg explained.[1] Around its annual Connect conference, the company announced it would take the name Meta Platforms (Meta) in a bold rebranding effort to make its brand and future platforms synonymous with the emerging digital worlds known as the *Metaverse*.

Over thirty years, the Metaverse has evolved from the pages of science fiction into a guiding corporate business strategy for the future of the internet and human connectivity. The term first appeared in Neal Stephenson's 1992 novel *Snow Crash*. The author defined the Metaverse as a global virtual-reality-based network that allows users to communicate digitally and conduct business from a distance. At the time of *Snow Crash*'s publication, the first iteration of the internet via dial-up connectivity was just emerging across the United States.

Today, the Metaverse's meaning revolves around the next iteration of the internet, a coming convergence of physical and virtual worlds. Unlike Web 1.0, which centered on content-destination personal sites, and Web 2.0, which is faster, collaborative, and focused on user trust, Web 3.0 will provide content anytime, anywhere, through any channel or device and will personalize the online experience.

The Metaverse—a critical part of Web 3.0—will allow humans to work, shop, and socialize in virtual environments just as immersive and engaging as the real world. It will drastically alter every industry it touches, from gaming and retail to entertainment and education. Overall, the Metaverse has the potential to be a transformative ecosystem worth at least $10 trillion by 2030, according to Citi,[2] while Epyllion CEO Matthew Ball projects it could reach $30 trillion.[3]

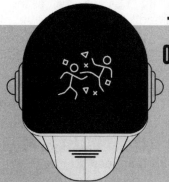

THE METAVERSE—A CRITICAL PART OF WEB 3.0—WILL ALLOW HUMANS TO WORK, SHOP, AND SOCIALIZE IN VIRTUAL ENVIRONMENTS JUST AS IMMERSIVE AND ENGAGING AS THE REAL WORLD.

Naturally, every Silicon Valley tech company is staking its claim today.

MARK ZUCKERBERG'S METAVERSE VISION

Mark Zuckerberg—who famously built Facebook's empire through an aggressive growth strategy—wanted to replicate his social media success and quickly capture market share in the burgeoning Metaverse. Many Wall Street analysts and tech executives had anticipated Zuckerberg's gambit given the CEO had telegraphed the rebranding months prior.

In July 2021, he told media outlet The Verge that Facebook "will effectively transition from people seeing us as primarily being a social media company to being a metaverse company."[4] Then, in September 2021, Zuckerberg promoted the leader of Facebook's Reality Labs, Andrew Bosworth, to chief technology officer.

The promotion replaced Mike Schroepfer, who had held the CTO position for eight years,[5] and signaled a dramatic shift in corporate strategy. For years, Reality Labs quietly managed Facebook's virtual reality (VR), augmented reality (AR), and brain-to-machine hardware projects. Now, Reality Labs would sit at the forefront of Zuckerberg's ambitious plans.

"From now on, we're going to be metaverse first, not Facebook first," Zuckerberg said in an introductory video announcing the transition.[6]

In a complementary letter to shareholders, the CEO envisioned a future where billions of people would spend their time traversing the Metaverse, enhancing their job productivity, playing games with friends, and socializing on existing Facebook networks.

"In the metaverse, you'll be able to do almost anything you can imagine—get together with friends and family, work, learn, play, shop, create—as well as completely new experiences that don't really fit how we think about computers or phones today," he wrote. He concluded that Facebook would allocate resources and energy to the Metaverse "more than any other company in the world."[7]

Now, before we dive deeper into this, I want to explain the concept of *walled gardens*. In a garden surrounded by walls, it is impossible for anything to escape. That is a proper metaphor for the technology sector. Companies like Meta have built walled gardens for their industries. Here they can control everything that happens within the ecosystem. They make the rules, they set up payment services that only benefit them, and they wall off content—making it impossible to access such content outside of their platforms.

At the onset of Facebook, Zuckerberg had wanted to create an open platform that allowed users to share content anywhere in the world. The basic idea was that the company could share as much content as possible and improve consumer choice.

But things changed with time. Zuckerberg wanted to focus on keeping more control in the world of Facebook. The company started to remove features that made it possible to share content outside of the Facebook platform. By default, it feels a lot more authoritarian in the approach. Zuckerberg and his team set the rules and reaped the financial benefits of a more closed-off system.

Within the world of big tech, regulators and governments have been quite wary of such business practices. Primarily, regulators are concerned about privacy, data protection, and a lack of competition. Governments around the globe want to ensure that consumers' privacy is safe. They don't want companies to have too much power in what users see, how users access information, and what users share.

GOVERNMENTS AROUND THE GLOBE WANT TO ENSURE THAT CONSUMERS' PRIVACY IS SAFE. THEY DON'T WANT COMPANIES TO HAVE TOO MUCH POWER IN WHAT USERS SEE, HOW USERS ACCESS INFORMATION, AND WHAT USERS SHARE.

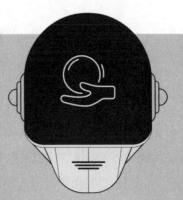

Meta Platforms is one of the most powerful players in the tech industry. Regulators have argued the company hasn't done enough to stop the spread of misinformation. But Meta is just one of the big players; we can't blame everything on Zuckerberg.

That said, after assessing Facebook's transition, I believe Zuckerberg's rebranding and multibillion-dollar capital expenditures around Metaverse projects could go down as one of the worst corporate strategy decisions of the twenty-first century. And not solely because of the poor financial outcome.

Following Facebook's transition to Meta Platforms, Zuckerberg pushed his chips across the table. He told investors that the company's 2021 profitability would crater by $10 billion and that Meta's hefty investments into Reality Labs would follow well into the future.[8]

It's unclear how much money Meta Platforms will spend developing Zuckerberg's Metaverse vision. However, venture capitalist Chamath Palihapitiya estimated that the company had spent $25 billion on Reality Labs between 2021 and 2022. Palihapitiya further estimated on an episode of the *All-In* podcast in November 2022 that Meta Platforms may end up spending $250 billion on its Metaverse ambitions over a decade.[9]

That figure—inflation adjusted—would rival the U.S. government's total investment in the Apollo space program from 1960 to 1973.[10]

In October 2022, the *New York Times* reported that Meta Platforms executives had battled openly around the company's ambitions. One senior Meta Platforms official complained that the amount of company capital poured into Zuckerberg's Metaverse projects had made him "sick to [his] stomach."[11]

Yet for all that investment, the results have underwhelmed. Critics have panned Zuckerberg's Metaverse initiatives, citing uninspiring graphics, clunky features, and the lack of a cohesive vision. Employees have publicly complained that Meta's projects are subject to the CEO's ever-changing whims.[12] And shareholders have taken the biggest hit.

Between the official 2021 announcement and the end of 2022, Meta Platforms stock plunged by 66 percent.[13] In that time, the company's market capitalization declined from north of $1 trillion to roughly $300 billion. Though it eventually recovered in 2023, the initial decline was primarily influenced by the company's stunning cash burn rate.[14]

Zuckerberg later said he'd been overly optimistic about the global transition to e-commerce and digital adoption in the wake of the COVID-19 epidemic, so much so that he subsequently increased capital expenditures for his Metaverse projects during the pandemic.

By November 2022, likely under pressure from activist and outspoken shareholders, Zuckerberg announced that the company would need to cut 13 percent or 11,000 members of its workforce in an effort to "become more capital efficient." In a letter to employees, Zuckerberg blamed shifts in e-commerce trends, the macroeconomic slump, rising competition, and weakening advertising revenue. "I got this wrong, and I take responsibility for that," he wrote about managing his company's balance sheet.[15]

Yet, for all the articles and stories covering Meta Platforms' sputtering transition, most analysts and journalists still fail to recognize Zuckerberg's one fundamental error—a simple truth that fueled all this chaotic spending and ever-shifting corporate strategy.

Zuckerberg has gotten everything wrong about the basic ecosystem required to ensure the Metaverse's future success.

And no estimated $250 billion investment could ever change that.

THE BATTLE FOR METAVERSE DOMINANCE

Meta Platforms isn't alone in driving a corporate Metaverse strategy strapped to an executive's vision or ego. In an October 2022 blog post, Jeff Teper, president of Microsoft Collaborative Apps and Platforms, bragged of an industrial Metaverse centered on Microsoft's HoloLens augmented reality headsets.[16] The blog's accompanying graphics featured images of legless avatars sitting around a floating table and staring at a virtual screen titled "New Employee Orientation." Microsoft's imagined work-Metaverse is *hardly* imaginative.

From the United States to China, Canada to South Korea, multinational tech giants are stepping over each other in a battle for Metaverse dominance. If a company's stock is found in the S&P 500 Information Technology sector, it likely featured a Metaverse strategy update in its 2021 annual report, focusing on building market share and maximizing revenue. That said, Zuckerberg is the only executive to fully align his company (he controls 57 percent of Meta Platforms' voting shares) directly with the Metaverse.[17]

To his credit, he has presented the future of the Metaverse and made the concept a household name. Zuckerberg naturally understands the importance of social networks in the Metaverse's future. He has acted as an advocate to display the possibilities of the Metaverse. And he has signaled that Meta Platforms will be only one among many participants in the Metaverse's evolution.

It's no secret that Zuckerberg aims to dominate and centralize Meta's power in the Metaverse, to set industry policies and standards that capture market share, and to extract as much revenue as possible for his shareholders.

I don't believe that Zuckerberg will ultimately succeed in these goals.

To understand what makes Zuckerberg's Metaverse vision so prone to failure, one must start in the boardroom of any public company. By default, Zuckerberg's corporate role executes a fiduciary duty to his shareholders. This responsibility makes it quite difficult for the company to invest tens of billions of dollars or promote open-source software without generating solid returns for its investors. This duty forces Zuckerberg to prioritize his shareholders and platforms over a burgeoning decentralized ecosystem.

Zuckerberg is a technology visionary and ardent supporter of the Metaverse—this fundamental responsibility has shaped Meta Platforms' corporate approach. One cannot fault Zuckerberg for this thinking, as it is baked into the mind of every CEO and venture capitalist who funded the first and second iterations of the internet. However, as I'll explain, Meta is not set up from the alignment and financial perspectives to become what Zuckerberg wants: the dominant player in the Metaverse's future.

Let's look at three critical factors that prove my point.

First, the company's rebranding represents a troubling effort to establish Meta as a technology gatekeeper to the Metaverse. Second, Meta's emphasis on the role of its virtual reality headsets as a gateway to its Metaverse experience acts as a severely limiting access point. And third, the centralized nature of Meta Platforms will likely drive the company out of favor among content creators as it seeks to maximize revenue and exploit developer relationships. Let's unpack all three.

UNLOCKING THE GATES

We'll start with the issue of gatekeeping. Harvard Business School will tell you that a consumer-facing company's ultimate success is building a brand synonymous with a product category. The finest example of this phenomenon in the twenty-first century is Google. The search giant is no longer just a brand name.

Google is now a verb that is synonymous with searching for information on a web browser. In many cases, users might even google terms in the search engines of the company's rivals, Bing, Yahoo!, or DuckDuckGo.

Of course, Google isn't the only success story of brand association. Travel to the state of Georgia and you'll find that nearly every soft drink is called a *Coke*—even if the restaurant offers you an RC Cola or a Pepsi. Other successful examples include the brands Jacuzzi, Crock-Pot, Bubble Wrap, Kleenex, Q-tips, Band-Aid, and even PowerPoint (created by Microsoft).

Unfortunately, Meta Platforms' recent name change feels like something ripped directly from a business school textbook to *force* brand association. At its core, the problem is that one company cannot and will not own the development or gatekeeping of the Metaverse. Thinking back to the first iterations of the internet, I'd argue that Meta's corporate approach is reminiscent of America Online (AOL).

This clunky, dial-up online platform emerged to prominence in the late 1990s yet collapsed into oblivion with the emergence of high-speed internet, decentralized protocols, and the lack of requirements needed to sign in online. Eventually, you no longer required an AOL account to reach the internet or create an email account. As developers unrelated to AOL's strategy built the broader ecosystem linked to Internet 1.0, you just needed an internet connection through any connected devices.

In the early days, many people believed the walled garden of AOL *was* the internet. Over time, these users discovered that AOL was merely one small neighborhood of a broader online world. AOL positioned itself as the entire internet experience when all its users really needed was a connection—an on-ramp—giving them access to the entire internet superhighway. In the same way, Zuckerberg wants Meta to *be* the Metaverse, when really all its users need is a way to access what Meta and every other company is building in the *wider* Metaverse.

Meta Platforms' vision originates from the mind and strategy of one person, Mark Zuckerberg, who believed a successful transition from social networking to the Metaverse was inevitable. That said, we know neither one person nor one company can create or establish the entire ecosystem of the Metaverse, just as America Online could not contain the expansion of the internet or develop its full possibilities. A top-down, corporate approach would stifle Metaverse innovation, limiting the power and reach of new and emerging technologies. Meta Platforms is largely trying to build its version of the Metaverse for others based on what its developers and Zuckerberg think its constituents want. The optimal Metaverse will be created and designed by these same constituents without centralized restrictions or arbitrary standards set by one company or a few companies together (a duopoly or digital oligarchy).

This brings me to my second point: Meta Platforms' centralized focus on VR as the primary access point to the Metaverse is severely limiting. The company famously purchased VR headset manufacturer Oculus for $1 billion in 2016 and quickly cornered the market in that industry. According to IDC's Worldwide Quarterly Augmented and Virtual Reality Headset Tracker, Meta Quest represents 90 percent of the VR headset market share. The second leading VR hardware company—ByteDance's Pico—represents just 4.5 percent of the headset market.[18]

It isn't surprising that Zuckerberg would attempt to leverage Meta's social networking dominance to promote VR. Facebook comprised 64.3 percent of the social media market share (by share of visits) in October 2022, and its wholly owned Instagram platform represented an additional 8.8 percent. Those combined figures represent nearly three-fourths of all social media activity.[19]

So, marrying the company's two dominant channels makes sense from a microeconomic perspective. Zuckerberg's Metaverse strategy and projects quickly took on a centralized, corporate approach to focus operations, standards, and communities around VR. When announcing Meta's intentions to become a Metaverse company, Zuckerberg said it would sell VR headsets at or below cost—effectively subsidizing its hardware.[20]

VR headsets are only one screen, and it's a massive assumption that users would adopt one central entry point to the Metaverse. In addition, VR headsets can be clunky, expensive, and even nauseating for some users. They also represent a severe limitation to the technological capabilities of the Metaverse—which extends beyond one screen to multiple ones, including cell phones, televisions, desktop monitors, digital projectors, and much more. As I'll later explain, new technologies and touchpoints continue to emerge—and will create an immersive Metaverse experience.

Meanwhile, the world that Zuckerberg has touted using VR headsets is rather uninspiring compared to my vision of the Metaverse's potential. The *real* Metaverse is an immersive and natural experience that revolves around the user—allowing them to travel through the virtual and physical worlds on their preferred devices anytime, anywhere.

THE *REAL* METAVERSE IS AN IMMERSIVE AND NATURAL EXPERIENCE THAT REVOLVES AROUND THE USER —ALLOWING THEM TO TRAVEL THROUGH THE VIRTUAL AND PHYSICAL WORLDS ON THEIR PREFERRED DEVICES ANYTIME, ANYWHERE.

Look at how Zuckerberg described the interaction between two users in the Metaverse—which revolves around VR hardware, *not the user*:

> In the future, instead of just doing this over a phone call, you'll be able to sit as a hologram on my couch, or I'll be able to sit as a hologram on your couch, and it'll actually feel like we're in the same place, even if we're in different states or hundreds of miles apart. So, I think that is really powerful.[21]

Wow. Imagine sitting on a virtual couch while wearing a Meta Quest VR headset. That's not very exciting.

The limitations don't end there. Zuckerberg regularly touts VR experiences catered toward virtual business meetings and operations. Meta Platforms has marketed Metaverse experiences to include "private virtual office[s]," a "magic shared space," and a "truly infinite office."[22]

In Meta Platforms' *Workplace* blog, the Metaverse sounds more like productivity software than an immersive experience that transforms industries, empowers brands, or enriches humanity. The company has touted Meta Quest as a tool to help employees boost multitasking capabilities in a virtual setting.[23] If that doesn't put you to sleep, the corporate strategy will.

Yet, on the surface, it all makes sense. Meta Platforms is seeking ways to generate revenue quickly. Much to the chagrin of some users, it has even attempted to experiment with in-headset advertising.[24] The company appears to be falling back on its initial successes, trying to leverage advertising dollars where possible.

The centralization of Meta's strategy around its headsets brings me to my third and final point: the nature of Meta Platforms' centralized strategies limits the potential for users and businesses to maximize their revenue and social potential in the Metaverse.

This factor—most likely—will be the reason why Meta Platforms' efforts fail.

In addition to centralizing its strategy around VR, the company needs to address the fundamental challenges linked to human resources and payment systems in the Metaverse.

The centralized nature of Meta Platforms reestablishes the legacy problems facing developers, artists, and others regarding revenue generation in today's e-commerce world. As I've noted, Zuckerberg's sensibility to shareholders is to maximize the company's value and revenue. Nowhere is this more evident than in human capital and compensation.

Meta will try to centralize key platforms under its brand, but the most important experiences and the most valuable Metaverse assets—which I call Metasites—will be developed by an independent group of people who think they work for themselves and believe they work for themselves. As the evolution of the Metaverse creates greater power and profit potential for independent developers and collaborators, Meta Platforms will face a massive creative problem around the company's revenue share model.

Zuckerberg wants to maximize profit for shareholders. However, this strategy requires extracting as much value from employees and creators as possible. Those individuals won't want to work for Meta Platforms. They'll want to create projects themselves, and they'll want to make money independently of Meta Platforms.

In the past, developers were forced to create projects aligned with the ecosystem of a large technology company like Meta Platforms or Apple. They either went to work for the company (in some cases, making their projects the intellectual property of those businesses) or they had to build and sell their products and services on centralized app stores. That won't be the case in the future.

The advent of blockchain technology and decentralized payment systems can obliterate Meta Platforms' market power. The nature of these payment systems provides greater financial incentives for independent developers as well as more intellectual and creative freedom. People will keep their data and payment information on the blockchain and will be spared the annoyance of keying them in time after time. This will also provide for greater security and privacy. In addition, Meta Platforms and its rivals will no longer be able to influence price decisions, limit a developer's audience, or interfere in collaboration or commerce between independent parties.

In my opinion, Meta Platforms' challenges—its stubbornness, centralization, and top-down approach—are good news. You see,

Zuckerberg's vision teaches us not only how corporate interests can limit the Metaverse's potential but also what the Metaverse *shouldn't be* for developers, creatives, users, and entrepreneurs.

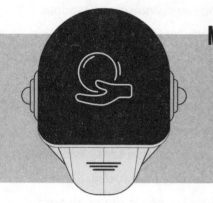

META PLATFORMS' CHALLENGES —ITS STUBBORNNESS, CENTRALIZATION, AND TOP-DOWN APPROACH—ARE GOOD NEWS.

And once we see what the Metaverse shouldn't be, we reveal its limitless potential.

THE FUTURE IS DECENTRALIZATION

I previously worried that the names Mark Zuckerberg, Facebook, and Meta Platforms might synonymize the Metaverse. The social media giant's effort to align its brand and establish entry points through Meta Quest accompanied a massive public relations and advertising blitz. It can be hard for independent content creators and consumers to battle against the influence of a $1 trillion company. And Meta Platforms' reach extends beyond e-commerce. As the Metaverse goes mainstream, I expect Meta Platforms, Microsoft, Amazon, and other tech giants to expand their reach and influence in politics, regulatory oversight, celebrity culture, and related secondary factors in this ecosystem.

I'd long predicted that traditional abuses of today's internet and e-commerce system would creep into the Metaverse. Centralized companies like Meta Platforms and Apple are building infrastructure and constructing gates around the Metaverse. Microsoft has already aligned its stack of legacy technologies—including its Windows operating system, Azure Cloud computing, Teams communication network, LinkedIn professional network, and Xbox gaming system—into a partnership with Meta Platforms' Quest headsets.[25] These companies will try to use gates (like VR headsets and hardware or subscription services) to charge entrance fees to participants with the goal of customer capture.

Meanwhile, I expect these companies will *try* to push some of the best creative developers and programmers into exclusive, non-competitive agreements to build the centralized Metaverse visions of their tech executives. I further anticipate these centralized tech giants will repeat previous efforts to create app stores and their own standards that siphon revenue from content creators. While it may not be intentional, they will continue building frameworks that stifle creativity and limit intellectual passions.

They just can't help themselves.

And, like America Online, their efforts should ultimately stumble and fall out of favor with users—leading to new leaders in a more decentralized future.

It's important to note that Zuckerberg isn't the only voice in the Metaverse. In fact, one should commend the initial vision of Epic Games CEO, Tim Sweeney, who laid out his grand vision for the Metaverse in December 2022:

Over the next few years, what we're going to be doing at Epic is bringing these pieces together into something that comes closer and closer to the metaverse from science fiction. Not the dystopian version of the metaverse from science fiction. But the really positive versions where you and your friends get together into a real-time 3D social experience and can explore the whole world.[26]

At the core of this goal, he said that a successful Metaverse would be "the creation of all of humanity's best content creators from all walks of life."[27] Absolutely. Not the centralized world that allows only a handful of people to create and decide what's possible. Like Sweeney, I envision a place where people are provided the tools to thrive and create experiences that excite them, brands that unite them, and ideas that ignite them.

I oppose the centralized legacy model of today's internet. I disliked it so much that my team built a company called Xsolla. Our business model is independent and decentralized, and it puts developers and creative minds first. Our mission is to help emerging video game creators access investment capital, leverage development tools, and maximize revenue.

Today, we're winning in the video game sector against the more prominent, more centralized players. We're now establishing a vision for business development in the next generation of the internet (Metaverse), video games, and content creation. And I assure you, the centralized corporate efforts around the Metaverse cannot and will not dominate.

I ENVISION A PLACE WHERE PEOPLE ARE PROVIDED THE TOOLS TO THRIVE AND CREATE EXPERIENCES THAT EXCITE THEM, BRANDS THAT UNITE THEM, AND IDEAS THAT IGNITE THEM.

Given the unlimited potential of the Metaverse, I don't want young programmers, artists, visionaries, or consumers to think of it as another corporate profit center. I don't want anyone to perceive it as another platform that siphons time and money from content producers and leaves them with pennies on the dollar for their hard work and vision.

I also don't want creative, energetic entrepreneurs and content experts to settle for jobs at Meta Platforms or other Silicon Valley companies, developing the Metaverse or giving away their passion projects to corporate entities. Too often, creative innovators work for hire at these massive technology companies with little upside for their personal ideas or projects. I don't view these employer-creative relationships as a productive means of creative expression. There is a better model, and we're working toward it daily.

RE-ENVISIONING THE METAVERSE

In this book, I'll share a radically different vision of the Metaverse.

My vision is transformational and aspirational compared to the one you'll see on television, experience at industry conferences, or hear from my fellow technology CEOs.

I'll showcase the limitless potential of this future ecosystem as it unites emerging and legacy brands, unleashes unforgettable consumer experiences, enriches humanity and cultures, equalizes global opportunities, and offers access to the most immersive technologies available (today and in the future).

My Metaverse vision empowers and rewards content creators across the globe, from developers in South America to artists in Europe to lonely scientists in Antarctica who'd love some company (virtually) from people worldwide. It accelerates development and revenue potential for anyone—including musicians, independent filmmakers, and business owners—seeking a new channel to expand their brand and reach new customers. It also builds hope and opportunity in education for children and adults worldwide.

I'm incredibly optimistic about the Metaverse's future.

I want everyone to know they can develop products and experiences they love—without corporate tech's overreach. Anyone can carve out their place in this digital horizon and enrich themselves as they choose. The new Metasites I'll discuss (the next generation of business and personal websites) will provide creative minds *everywhere* with the chance to tell their stories, discover their motivations as entrepreneurs, and explore their passions.

This is a place for *everyone* financially, socially, and creatively.

The internet has become the great equalizer of this world—and the Metaverse will be an even greater extension of this phenomenon.

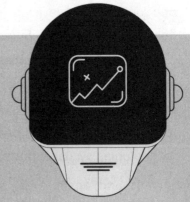

THE INTERNET HAS BECOME
THE GREAT EQUALIZER OF
THIS WORLD—AND
THE METAVERSE WILL BE
AN EVEN GREATER EXTENSION
OF THIS PHENOMENON.

I know all too well how powerful these developing platforms can be. I grew up poor in Siberia, Russia, and I owe a massive debt to the creative minds and technology communities that helped equalize opportunity—which eventually allowed me to develop a next-generation platform in Xsolla that rewards rather than exploits content creators. I anticipate that the Metaverse will create a digital gold rush for content creators, and we want to be the ones handing them shovels and picks so they can get to work and build the decentralized Metaverse of the future.

No single company can develop every mechanism or establish the standards on which this new world known as the Metaverse operates. The Metaverse will accelerate a decentralized movement that shifts away from Silicon Valley's control and places the experience, profit potential, and freedom into the hands of creative communities.

As I'll explain, for nearly two decades, platforms like YouTube (owned by Alphabet's Google) and apps like Apple Music, Spotify, and Amazon Prime have paid musicians, filmmakers, and producers fewer and fewer royalties for the same or *even more* work. Modern music and creative royalty systems that compensate artists and producers are broken. The Metaverse can correct these historical failures and increase profit potential for creators.

For future users of the Metaverse, I'll also outline much different functionality and technology than you may have seen commercially. The Metaverse will transform the future of almost every consumer-facing industry: fashion, healthcare, entertainment, and, again, every element of consumer goods. It will alter business-to-business industries and enhance training for surgeons, dentists, and next-generation employment. It will fuel educational advancements and city planning. And I *really* hope that it will become a revolutionary driver of charity and nonprofit efforts in fundraising and showcasing achievements in building a better future for countless causes.

If anything, Meta Platforms' difficult 2022 proved that the Metaverse cannot and should not have gatekeepers or technological limitations. It cannot and will not be confined to expensive Meta Quest hardware, Apple's Vision Pro headsets, Microsoft's HoloLens, or Google Glasses that cost consumers thousands of dollars. The Metaverse's backbone exists through the interface of video game elements on *any* screen. Users will connect to the Metaverse via their phones, desktops, televisions, and even digital "caves." They will enter this interactive universe and seamlessly move from Metasite to Metasite in a manner that cultivates their senses. I expect the immersive digital cave—which I'll describe in greater detail later in the book—will be more natural and immersive than any future VR experience through Meta Quest hardware.

In addition, the Metaverse will operate on a far different financial model than today's internet. Blockchain technology (previously unavailable on previous iterations of the internet) will enable content creators to generate more money for their ideas and products, cutting out corporate middlemen and gatekeepers. Such decentralization of the Metaverse combined with blockchain technology (transactions, payments, tokenization, movement of items on the blockchain, and customization) will allow users, artists, and entrepreneurs to make a living and boost their earning power.

That's because consumers will also interact with content creators, brands, and businesses in radical new ways. They'll be able to purchase and take "tangible" items with them and build a digital inventory. They will experience an interactive, multilayered world that transcends our current internet—enabling unforgettable socialization, personalized education, product demonstrations, and e-commerce experiences. The Metaverse will help engineer a radically different world from what we know today and will not be limited by the centralized plans of a digital oligarchy.

In this book, I'll also encourage you to think about what you want from the Metaverse. If you're a consumer or student, do you want to sit in Mark Zuckerberg's digital cubicle or virtual office meetings all day while completing work tasks?

Or do you want to fly above Manhattan with the ease of Superman?

The *real* Metaverse can already take you across the world's skies.

Do you want to sit on a friend's couch and play checkers with their digital avatar?

Or do you want to stand inside the Sistine Chapel, look up, and see God's hand touching man (all from your living room, and all without needing a Meta Quest headset)?

That experience will be within *your* reach.

Consider a future where a Google or DuckDuckGo query won't just show you pictures and offer text around the subject of your search. The digital cave that I'll describe will immerse you in the search, make 3D lions or dinosaurs appear in your room, or take you to the steps of the Great Temple of Petra in Jordan. You'll explore deep space's once-impossible reaches and the oceans' inhabitable depths. Users can immerse themselves anywhere—from Fenway Park in Boston to Times Square in New York City. You'll attend lectures at Oxford University and concerts at the Sydney Opera House. You'll witness *and* relive history. You'll have the chance to sit "live" ringside at today's greatest boxing matches or travel back in time to experience the legendary fights between Muhammad Ali and George Foreman from *inside* the ring.

I'll also show you how the Metaverse will evolve, one technology at a time. Most of the technologies required to build this future exist today. Others will develop as new programs and protocols advance. Remember, there was a time when the platforms of Instagram and Snapchat could not exist due to technological limitations. New iterations of the iPhone and other smartphones enabled engineers to build these platforms. I'll preview the emerging technologies that will act as foundations for unlimited, immersive applications, ecosystems, and experiences. I'll discuss the roles of internet-hosting providers, website developers, and cloud computing and infrastructure engineers, and the ongoing need for advanced networking and hardware. I'll also talk about the Metaverse entrepreneurs who will develop Metasites and the positive impact that Metasites will have on every business.

Again, the best part of this future is that anyone can take part in this Metaverse revolution—an estimated $10 trillion to $30 trillion opportunity by 2030.[28] Anyone can create, share, search, explore, and enrich themselves as the Metaverse grows. Anyone can build a business and brand and make money every day. This book not only shares that potential but also serves as a guide to discovering and achieving economic and personal success in the Metaverse.

Before we discuss all the incredible opportunities and solutions created by the Metaverse, I want to show you how much technology and the internet have changed my life. I'll quickly explain why I built a unique platform that placed power back into the hands of content creators in my favorite industry: the video game sector.

I think you'll find this story empowering, and I hope it kick-starts ideas on boosting your brand while opening your mind to the Metaverse's exciting possibilities.

CHAPTER 2

MY STORY: FROM SIBERIA TO SHERMAN OAKS

When I was fourteen, the cable network MTV (Music Television) came to Russia.

Over the ensuing years, the music channel greatly influenced me. Yes, I dyed my hair blond and discovered new music that's still on my iPhone. The network really became a window to wonderland. To some people, MTV is just a reality show network. In Russia, we had nothing like it. What I saw on those shows and videos wasn't close to my reality.

From the beach parties in California on the show *Laguna Beach* to the diverse communities in Manhattan and other cities on *The Real World*, I loved it all. Each day, my school friends and I watched MTV from Russia's cold, dense regions and dreamed of something else. We dreamed of hosting a crazy party like the movie characters in *American Pie* and *Can't Hardly Wait*, with big, beautiful pools and red plastic cups.

In my reality, I spent nearly three hours each day on a beaten-up public bus going to and from school. I couldn't even dream of a Sony Walkman—the *cassette tape* version, not even the compact disc (CD) version. I was fortunate to own a $7 portable radio. And until I turned eighteen—in 2002—I had neither a computer nor internet access.

Those American shows and films presented a motivation for a better life. They made a young man from Siberia dream of California and work with content creators who transform films, music, and games from simple ideas into award-winning art forms.

More than twenty years later, my life has changed in ways I couldn't have imagined. I founded Xsolla, a global financial platform for video game developers. Now, I've set my focus on the third iteration of the internet—the Metaverse. We've moved from the first iteration of paid, dial-up web platforms like America Online and CompuServe. We'll soon move away from a centralized digital economy where consumers are reliant on large e-commerce giants like Amazon and music services like Spotify and Apple Music to purchase the products and services we want.

In February 2022, we announced X.LA, a community-driven organization that will maximize how content creators make money from their work in the Metaverse. We'll leverage blockchain and the next generation of revenue-sharing technologies to empower content creators worldwide.

That concept seems so far away from where my story began. It feels like a dream.

As you read this journey, I hope that you believe anything is possible. Because *anything* is. And when the Metaverse grows into its potential, I hope you'll have an opportunity to virtually see where I grew up and why I came to the US.

Most Americans have little understanding of the former Soviet Union or the oligarchical system that evolved after its collapse in

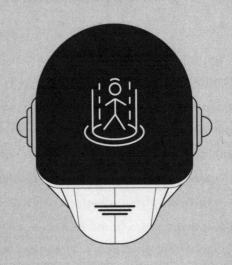

AS YOU READ THIS JOURNEY, I HOPE THAT YOU BELIEVE *ANYTHING* IS POSSIBLE. BECAUSE ANYTHING IS.

the 1990s. Today, most people see Russia through the leadership of President Vladimir Putin, who came to power in 2000. They may read headlines about the recent war in Ukraine and the decades-long political tensions between Russia and the United States.

But that's today.

I want to take you back *then*, back to when and where I was born.

It's the opposite of the Metaverse. It doesn't have many happy Hollywood endings.

MY LIFE LONG BEFORE THE METAVERSE

Imagine a place where private property is essentially banned. Imagine a place where speculating on real estate or turning a profit as a business owner could bring a lengthy jail sentence. Imagine a place where people give up on their dreams at an early age—where opportunity doesn't exist and the government can shut down any business, anytime, for political or personal reasons (or worse, without any reason at all).

That was life in the Soviet Union, or the Union of Soviet Socialist Republics (USSR).

My youth in the USSR was critical to my life's ups, downs, lessons, and failures. It was also central to establishing the mindset and vision that brought me to America.

As you'll learn, I love Los Angeles, New York, and San Francisco immensely. There is electricity to the creative grit that fills so many parts of the US. That entrepreneurial spirit was incredibly foreign to my family and the people where I grew up.

Even though I've written this book, it can be tough to put into words just how much I appreciate a free economy, twenty-first-century technology, and how welcoming the US is to entrepreneurs.

My hometown is Perm, Russia, a city of roughly one million people about 720 miles east of Moscow, the nation's capital. Perm sits near the Ural Mountains, right on the border of Europe and Asia. It's incredibly remote, on the edge of the endless, snowy Siberian forest.

If someone looked at a map of the former Soviet Union, they wouldn't find Perm on it. The government hid my town from the world. During World War II, military companies and other critical state-owned enterprises moved to the proximity of Perm. There were more than twenty state-owned companies in the region. The list of companies included artillery and shell producers, anti-tank missile and weapon manufacturers, and rifle and gunpowder makers.

In my early years, there was no Starbucks, no McDonald's, and no access to most Western music or entertainment. Perm was a place of government secrets and government influence. It wasn't a place that Soviet leaders wanted the world to see—and that made it even more difficult for young people to find their identity, drive, and life passions.

I'm serious about saying the Soviet government didn't want the world to see us. Even though Germany's military didn't plan to advance to Perm in World War II, the Russian government camouflaged the city's airbase. With so many state secrets, Perm unofficially became a closed city during and after the war. Foreigners couldn't visit for decades. The state removed Perm from Soviet maps. Even today, few people know about the city, its location, or its industrial importance to Russia's economy over the decades.

My grandmother, Alevtina, and my mother, Alla, worked in the dangerous Perm Gunpowder Plant for their entire careers. The company started in 1934 as a manufacturer of explosives for the mining sector. Today, it produces Grad and Smerch rocket launch systems for Russian troops.[29] Despite decades of vast government spending in the region, Perm wasn't a bastion of economic or entrepreneurial opportunity in the twentieth century.

After World War II, the US engaged in the Marshall Plan, which rebuilt Europe and exported capitalism. It also fueled the Cold War, a multi-decade standoff between American-influenced capitalism and Soviet-style socialism and communism worldwide.

I grew up in the latter system. In the Soviet economy, poverty was rampant. The economy relied on state spending—with a pittance in wages and cramped living conditions for most people. Under the system, the government constructed and provided free apartments to every family with children. The more children a family had, the larger the apartment would be. The challenge for many families was the limited housing supply and the subsequent waiting period for an apartment, which could often take years. My parents were young when they had me; my mother was twenty years old when she started working at the Perm Gunpowder Plant. Since my father appeared sporadically in our lives, it took four years for her to get our first state-sponsored apartment.

I want to paint a quick picture of the size of that apartment. In 2015, *USA Today* reported that the average hotel room in the US was 330 square feet.[30] In Los Angeles, a five-star hotel room might be 600 to 800 square feet. The average three-star hotel room at your typical Hilton or Marriott might be 300 square feet.

Our first apartment was 182 square feet, with an additional kitchen space that was 64 square feet. It was tight between my parents and me—and even tighter once my sister was born, which happened shortly after we moved in. Following her arrival, we lived there for another seven years.

A three-section wardrobe divided our main space into the kids' room and the living room. There were bunk beds in the kids' room for my sister and me. My parents slept on a sofa in the living room. They had a desk, an ironing board, and two televisions. The larger television didn't work; it served as a stand for a small black-and-white TV. The tiny space also crowded out my chance to pursue music. I'd wanted to play the piano, but we didn't have enough space or money for one. I had to play the accordion instead.

I *hated* the accordion.

As a poor child, I didn't have much. I'd visit construction zones and trash dumps on occasion. Sometimes I'd find broken toys, perfume, and hand cream. Other times, I'd find potato peelings. I was lucky once and found a copper wire. When I sold it, I purchased a *Teenage Mutant Ninja Turtles* comic book with the money. It was a prized possession.

When you're poor in Russia, basic necessities are luxuries that are hard to obtain.

My family didn't have toilet paper. We used newspaper and magazine pages—and since we didn't have a subscription, it was my job to locate discarded newspapers and magazines in our apartment building. Before we used them, I would read the stories from the media.

I have distinct memories of reading about the Soviet occupation of Afghanistan, the 1988 earthquake in Armenia, and the 1990s economic period after the Soviet system's collapse that became known as *privatization*.

MY FORMATIVE YEARS

As rampant as poverty was in the USSR, so too was alcoholism.

It's a disease that ultimately took my father's life in 2004. He lacked a permanent career and bounced around from odd job to odd job. He also struggled with long bouts of chronic addiction. I've said that his life was like a box of chocolates, except every second one had alcohol in it. I remember nights of him passing out on the floor. I remember my mother trying to wake him, even punching him.

My father was only twenty-two when I was born. He'd spent two years in compulsory military service. He would occasionally sober up for extended periods and might spend two years with us before disappearing for a while. My grandmother would convince him that death awaited him for his reckless drinking. He'd be clean for eighteen months and then fall into the same uncontrollable cycle.

Two tragic episodes of his drinking shaped my youth.

One day, I returned from a friend's house and asked my father to sharpen pencils for me. I handed him a knife from the kitchen. Moments later, my parents got into an argument and my father hit my mother with that knife. He would receive three years in jail for the incident. In the USSR, jail wasn't a place for redemption or correction, as it largely kept prisoners from expecting any future professional or social hope. I have few memories from that time, though I recall visiting him in jail on two occasions. He spent his time making and selling prison tattoos, and I learned how to play chess from another inmate.

The second event happened in 1998. After his time in jail, my father was sober for a few years. My mother, still employed at the Perm Gunpowder Plant, received a two-week river cruise vacation for our family. On the last day of the cruise, as part of a joke, several ship entertainers snuck vodka into a water sports competition. My father, without his knowledge, tasted the alcohol. It triggered another relapse. He wouldn't stop drinking again until he died in 2004.

As a result of his drinking, he was never a reliable presence in my life, although there are fond memories from time to time. That said, his drinking also shaped my family economically during one of the most critical periods of post-Soviet history.

My father's heartbreaking financial decisions—like so many other people who lived in Perm and other regions of Russia during the early 1990s—had consequences. They'd also shape some of the most important memories and lessons of my teenage years.

In 1991, the former Soviet Union collapsed. The most regarded images of that time typically center on the fall of the Berlin Wall in Germany, which separated friends and families under two systems for decades. In Perm and other remote Russian locations, economic liberalization (or privatization) was underway. At the time, there was public excitement about the process. More than

60 percent of Russians supported privatization.[31] This was a great undoing of communism—a shift from inefficient, state-owned businesses to private enterprises and *supposed* opportunity for everyone.

That shift wasn't what most people experienced.

This was an incredibly confusing time for anyone with little education who had spent decades living under a communist system. Between 1992 and 1994, Russia's government provided every citizen—including children like me (I was eight when this program started)—a voucher worth 10,000 rubles. It was money that people could use to buy properties or other assets. They might even start a business with the money.

At face value, 10,000 rubles was enough for someone to purchase two cars.

That wasn't explained well to the populace. Nor did they receive answers to even more straightforward questions like, "How do people use a voucher?" or "What is privatization?"

The majority of people didn't understand the concept of private property. Just years prior, anyone could go to jail for "speculation" if they made a small profit from buying and selling an asset. Now, they were supposed to understand the concepts of business and market economics. The ensuing events would facilitate the Russian oligarch class that still exists today. Across the country, there was a group of elite, educated professionals who had studied abroad at business schools in Europe and the United States. They understood economics—and they could take advantage of the average person's ignorance of the topic.

These "businessmen" would exchange certain goods that were worth far less than 10,000 rubles for other people's vouchers. For example, various businessmen would arrive in the city with two trucks full of vodka. They'd visit a farmers' market and trade two bottles of alcohol for one voucher worth 10,000 rubles. After they'd collected enough of these vouchers, a businessperson could use them to privatize an oil production facility or a refinery at a closed auction. Despite receiving vouchers worth 40,000 rubles, my family found no economic success in this privatization effort.

It shouldn't surprise you that my father exchanged his voucher for a bottle of vodka. He traded my voucher as well. He received a bicycle, which he gave to me, and more vodka for him. Meanwhile, my mother, who lacked financial education, invested two vouchers in a Ponzi scheme. She lost all the money.

It'd be easy to feel anger about these events.

I approached this outcome in a different manner. Instead, I asked myself, *What lessons could be taken from this period of privatization when so many businesspeople exploited their fellow citizens?*

The answer was simple: education would be critical to my future and success.

Even though she was a hard worker, my mother never advanced far in her career due to her lack of education. She chose a tough job to receive a pension as early as possible; at age forty-five, she received a $150 monthly pension. My mother's life was not easy on her.

She and my grandmother told me two things daily. First, uneducated work—like their roles at the gunpowder factory—was incredibly hard. And second, it was essential for me to get an education and a university diploma.

I would do so at any cost, even if it meant telling a life-changing lie.

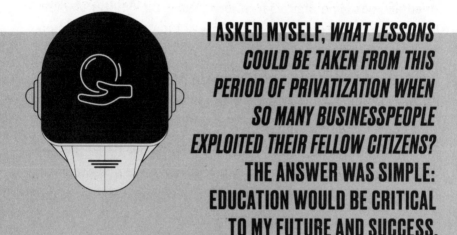

I ASKED MYSELF, *WHAT LESSONS COULD BE TAKEN FROM THIS PERIOD OF PRIVATIZATION WHEN SO MANY BUSINESSPEOPLE EXPLOITED THEIR FELLOW CITIZENS?* THE ANSWER WAS SIMPLE: EDUCATION WOULD BE CRITICAL TO MY FUTURE AND SUCCESS.

EDUCATION AS EMPOWERMENT

In the seventh grade, I finally had my own bedroom. My family moved to a much larger home in a much worse neighborhood near the Taiga Forest. I attended a new school, which didn't appeal to me. I remember fourteen-year-old students smoking cigarettes during the day and the same young people fighting at the discotheque at night. To give you a sense of the new world around me, consider this: the father of one of my classmates tried to sell me fake vodka that he made from tap water and grain alcohol. I decided to leave the school and try a military boarding academy.

It wouldn't take me long to realize I had no interest in joining the Russian military.

Still, this experience was a huge turning point in my life. While at the academy, a teacher recognized my love for and skills in mathematics. She started to tutor me and take me to city-level math contests. It was rare for a student from the military school to participate in these competitions, and even rarer for such a student to win them. I won a few, which helped the teacher get an award and a bonus. Honestly, I was just happy that I had met and had access to a passionate tutor.

During this time, I also discovered that better education was possible. I learned about a school called Lyceum, which was the best in the city. I wanted to attend Lyceum, but there was just one problem: I was in tenth grade. In Russia, schools have eleven grades, and Lyceum only accepted applicants for both the tenth and eleventh grades. When I inquired about applying and repeating tenth grade, an administrator said, "Our country is not that rich to teach you twice."

I wouldn't take no for an answer. I had to take a risk. So, I doctored my application and claimed to be younger than I was. Thankfully, no one fact-checked my application. When I passed the Lyceum entrance exam, I'd beaten twenty other students for my seat. This experience redefined my life and opened me up to opportunities and experiences I'd never witnessed.

When I walked into class on the first day at Lyceum, I was easily the worst-dressed student and possibly the poorest too.

Believe it or not, I was thrilled.

No one smoked cigarettes.

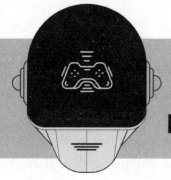

THIS EXPERIENCE REDEFINED MY LIFE AND OPENED ME UP TO OPPORTUNITIES AND EXPERIENCES I'D NEVER WITNESSED.

No one fought.

Plus, it was a big school with multiple buildings and twenty-two classrooms. It had a unique feel, like the school I'd seen on the television show *Beverly Hills, 90210*.

Lyceum was where the mayor's son and a chicken factory owner's daughter worked together and became friends. Several students in my class had spent a year in the US as part of an exchange program. I met alumni who went on to graduate from American universities. This instantly sparked my interest in the US education system—which I didn't yet know I'd ultimately attend.

It also helped me find my first mentor. If there is one person to whom I owe the most for my ultimate success in education, it is my math professor, Anatoly Prokopovich Ivanov.

At Lyceum, we studied math for four hours every day, and Ivanov was the author of the nationwide test system. He designed tests with thirty questions that were almost impossible to solve in sixty minutes. Despite the complexity, we'd try and learn to complete those problems.

I liked math sprint matches and became even more obsessed with multi-hour math competitions, which felt like sports matches. Working with Ivanov helped me reach my full potential in mathematics. I would go on to test among the top five students in the city and receive a scholarship from Perm State University.

This period of high school was critical to my development. By 2002, Russia had changed immensely. MTV arrived in 1998, but it reached peak influence four years later. On the weekends, I frequented Bolid Dance Planet, a dance hall inspired by New York's Studio 54. I'd dance there most nights until 6:00 a.m. That's because the first bus home didn't leave until 6:30 a.m. Even though I didn't make many friends at this club, I loved the techno music and the atmosphere. There was pure joy in the environment.

As I prepared for university, my parents divorced. They split the profits from the sale of our first apartment. When I moved back to Perm, I started to think about how to make money on a burgeoning technology known as the internet. That year, we purchased my first personal computer, my first car, and a sheepskin coat for my mother.

But as it does, life would quickly change and grow far more intense.

KEEPING MY EYE ON THE POTENTIAL

When I attended Perm State University, I realized how difficult it would be. At first, I couldn't follow the pace, and students had to learn under tremendous pressure. If students failed to pass their exams, they could reapply to the school but would have to pay their tuition. Those who lacked capital or couldn't pass the exams had to fulfill compulsory service in the Russian army. At the time, Russia was active in the Chechen War. I had no interest in military service, but I had childhood friends who were negatively affected physically and mentally by that war.

I'd need to ensure that I had money. I was fascinated by the potential of the new technology that had reached beyond the large cities of Moscow and St. Petersburg. In 2002, the internet found its way to my city. I could pay fifty cents per hour to access the Russian dial-up internet. However, it wasn't like America Online or the digital local area networks (LANs) that universities had in the US in the early 2000s. It was clunky and slow, and it would frequently disconnect or not work.

While many people complained about lack of opportunity in Russian business, I viewed the internet as the tool that leveled the playing field for me with anyone around the globe. I had extreme motivation, and I had an opportunity. The internet opened a new world for me. I quickly discovered that I could make more money on the internet than in the traditional labor market of Russia. I wasn't going online to read the news, download songs on Napster-like platforms, or get sports updates; I wanted to use the internet to make money and build successful businesses.

I VIEWED THE INTERNET AS THE TOOL THAT LEVELED THE PLAYING FIELD FOR ME WITH ANYONE AROUND THE GLOBE. I HAD EXTREME MOTIVATION, AND I HAD AN OPPORTUNITY. THE INTERNET OPENED A NEW WORLD FOR ME.

I viewed that fifty-cents-per-hour rate as my overhead cost for a better future. I quickly realized an opportunity existed in the processing of online transactions. By 2002, Russia experienced a financial technology boom that fueled the rise of small e-wallet companies. E-wallets are secure money apps or online platforms that allow users to make purchases through retailers, transfer money, send money to others, or exchange one currency (whether a foreign exchange or digital currency) for another.

At the time, few consumers had access to credit cards, and there was little regulation in the payment industry. My first initiative was registering every e-wallet available to get money in and out of a business.

Two burgeoning online sectors allowed me to do so: sports gambling and money exchanges. When it came to gambling, I had little interest in speculating on or even watching sports matches. Instead, I was looking to do something that most people hadn't considered. You see, various bookmakers had different odds online for different sports matches. I learned on internet forums how to arbitrage sporting events across multiple online sports books. I could make money without experiencing a net loss on a bet.

Here's how it worked: I could compare gambling lines (or odds) on Marafon, Russia's large bookmaker, to the odds offered on betfair.com, London's premiere sports gambling exchange. I discovered that when different bookmakers had different lines, I could make risk-free bets on both sides of the sporting event. In partnership with a developer from my school, I created my first sports arbitrage program online. I nicknamed it a "money-printing machine." I'd make another "money-printing machine" in a financial exchange that allowed users to purchase electronic money on WebMoney, a Russian payment settlement system, and change it to e-gold, a digital commodity platform that enabled users to own web currency denominated in grams of gold or other precious metals. I could also profit from consumers exchanging money in the other direction, between those platforms.

Naturally, those money machines required capital investment.

And so, too, would the next blessing in my life. Two years later, while attending a party, I met my wife, Yana. I fell in love with her instantly. Of course, I tried to look wealthier than I was at first.

Fortunately, I soon learned our relationship would last forever. She took a two-hour bus ride to meet my mother in her rundown apartment, and later she met and introduced herself to my father. We were very young when we married and moved in together; I was twenty-one, and she was nineteen.

Yana's father helped us renovate our first apartment, which I can only describe as a trash hole. I borrowed 700,000 rubles (or $20,000) to fund my businesses. I would pay an incredible 3.5 percent interest each month and use our apartment as collateral. This allowed me to feed my money machines and fund new projects, including the foundation of Xsolla.

Today, Xsolla is a business that helps video game developers access capital, creative tools, and resources. We empower them to build their audience, generate in-game payments, and access alternative payment systems for digital transactions.

But that wasn't Xsolla's origin story.

I consider Xsolla's official birthday to be July 15, 2005. That was the day I registered the domain 2pay.ru and founded 2pay, the predecessor of Xsolla.

Our first service allowed users to exchange one digital currency for another with a 1 percent fee. As we integrated new wallets, we started to add new virtual game currencies. It was a busy time. We launched a business with twenty different Russian browser games in six months. At the time, it felt like the company would make a fortune or go "to the moon"—as some US investors like to say.

There were humbling lessons along the way.

I relied heavily on developers to start, and one of my best developers would soon announce that he wanted to focus on his education. He asked me if I wanted to continue trading for him at night. When his trading program stopped working, he didn't fix it. That failure quickly eliminated an important revenue source. We ended our partnership.

Meanwhile, another developer took money from our "business wallet" without my authorization. That event ended another relationship and made me understand the importance of not only knowing your customers but also knowing your business partners.

Finally, I asked my sister to help manage our tennis trading. When she made a mistake in program configuration, I lost my bank. The situation that caused this was crazy. A tennis match was canceled due to rain, but my safe arbitrage bet between two betting sites was lost. One site decided that the match was canceled, while the other decided to count the score from when the rain ended the match. It was very painful to lose money back then.

Little did I know, I'd run out of money within six months.

It was a very challenging time. I sold my car. I left school. And remember, I owed an interest payment of 24,500 rubles (or $1,000 at the time) per month. If I didn't find a solution, I might lose that apartment my father-in-law had renovated.

I didn't panic. At first, I resigned to living on 4,000 rubles (or $163 at the time) per week with my wife. I visited my grandmother and introduced her to Yana. I wasn't shy about sharing my challenges. My grandmother told me, "If you spend 4,000 rubles per week, you will never be able to pay back your debt. How much do you think you can make?"

That conversation was meaningful—like so many others we had until she passed away. My grandmother was incredibly generous with her time and her apartment. During my school years, I'd frequently stay with her as she was just forty-five minutes from school compared to my mother's home, which was ninety minutes away. She always had my interest at heart.

It took more than two years and a lot of discipline to repay that 700,000-ruble loan *plus* interest. During that period, I also repurposed the business and put more time and effort into learning how to rebuild it. I didn't want to rely on developers or contractors. I had to learn how to run and operate my business all by myself. That time set the foundation for what Xsolla has become today—with offices all around the world.

After that conversation with my grandmother, I taught myself how to code and rebuilt my billing system from scratch. Everything I learned was freely available online, and the internet's vast educational resources helped equalize opportunity for me. I registered 2pay.ru as a corporation by myself. I wrote my first agreement with gamers by myself. I set up accounting. I established a phone system and 800 number. I managed all the virtual servers. This period—volatile as it was—was my founder's story, one that I know many entrepreneurs have experienced, with so many ups and down.

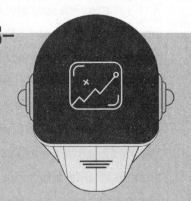

THIS PERIOD—VOLATILE AS IT WAS—WAS MY FOUNDER'S STORY, ONE THAT I KNOW MANY ENTREPRENEURS HAVE EXPERIENCED, WITH SO MANY UPS AND DOWN.

Then, a significant opportunity emerged between 2006 and 2008. During that time, many Russian consumers started to use bank cards. This brings me to another essential difference between the US and Russia, which was critical in developing my business.

In the US, contract law helps establish and enforce trust between businesses and consumers. Americans entrust their money to banks. They trust mobile companies as stewards of their data and privacy. Think about how much confidence consumers have in everything they buy in the US today. Some may even take it for granted. Americans trust that the person selling them a product is telling the truth and that services like banks will protect their interest. The US also has an incredible web of consumer protections and consumer advocates that Russia lacks.

In Russia, such trust doesn't really exist. People don't trust banks like they do in the US. As a result, the average Russian consumer used their banking cards only once or twice a month to withdraw their salary. And when mobile phones became more popular across Russia, consumers wouldn't link their phone bills to a bank account—which is common in America.

Instead, Russian consumers would prepay their phone bills. This created enormous opportunities for companies like QIWI, a Russian payment giant, to establish kiosks for users to pay bills with cash. Russian consumers would withdraw cash via their bank cards, insert the money into these kiosks, and then pay their phone and internet bills.

By the end of 2008, my company 2pay had aggregated two hundred games and 150 kiosk networks in Perm. These kiosks, like ATMs, were in every grocery store and were typically used to add to a mobile phone balance or pay a utility. My company utilized these kiosks to allow consumers to refill their gaming accounts with Free2Play games. Due to the blatant abundance of piracy, the only type of game experiences consumers were ready to pay for in Russia were free-to-play games.

These games were run from servers where cheating was impossible, so players were ready to spend a lot of money on in-game advantages. Perhaps this was one of the factors in Russia that was far ahead of its time compared to the US that created an unfair advantage for Xsolla.

My company was a success, yet I still dreamed of California and the potential on the other side of the world.

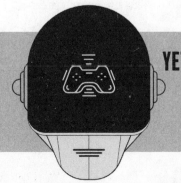

MY COMPANY WAS A SUCCESS, YET I STILL DREAMED OF CALIFORNIA AND THE POTENTIAL ON THE OTHER SIDE OF THE WORLD.

MY MOVE TO AMERICA

Long before I started Xsolla, I sincerely appreciated creative content—and American culture. As I mentioned earlier, following the privatization of Russia, my father exchanged my 10,000-ruble voucher for vodka and a bicycle. In his final two sober years, that bicycle was a terrific investment. We never had a car, and the bike allowed us to ride to a nearby lake where we would fish together. I have great memories of that quality one-on-one time with him.

Although he couldn't hold a job, he helped me develop a deep appreciation for Hollywood in 1997—one year before the arrival of MTV in Russia. At the time, my father worked as a VHS salesclerk for pirated videos. Long before CDs and DVDs, there were large, clunky video tapes. My father bought two VHS players and a label typing machine, which we would use to pirate copies of popular American films. While that is frowned on and illegal in the United States, I still think it was the coolest job my father ever had. Again, we didn't have much.

What's wild about this experience is that being a movie pirate was a high-pressure job. The label typing machine gave us only one chance to get the copy done correctly. Before my father would sell these tapes, I'd watch whatever movies I could. And when I saw them, they didn't seem real. They appeared to be part of a fantasy land, something that couldn't exist. So, you must imagine my joy when I first visited the United States.

My wife and I visited the US for the first time as tourists in 2009. As I learned about the US gaming industry and its potential at a San Francisco trade show, I found America was incredibly inviting.

I returned to that same trade show the following year with a booth for Xsolla and have revisited that event every year since.

With a growing business, I started to attract attention in the US. So, I made the leap and decided to move my family to America. We rented a one-bedroom apartment in San Francisco for the first year. In 2010, we established Xsolla's headquarters in Sherman Oaks, a neighborhood in Los Angeles, California. This helped us quickly scale our global operations.

It wasn't easy.

Moving from Russia to America was an adventure.

ADAPTING TO A NEW CULTURE

At first, California might as well have been the moon. I didn't understand English and had never formally learned the language. The US is also just one of three nations that doesn't use the metric system. So, I had to translate miles per hour from kilometers per hour. I had to learn the calculation between kilograms and pounds. I had to understand the difference between five feet, five yards, and five meters. This was a drastic change from a lifetime of measurements based on metric units.

There were also subtle nuances. I'd never been to a country where the address is on every building. I'd never been in a place with freedom of speech or Coca-Cola everywhere.

It's true that when you first arrive in the United States, it's hard to comprehend a place where every shelf in the grocery store isn't just covered, but products run two feet deep on those shelves. I could go on for hours about this subject, but that may be a different book.

It felt like a movie at times. I'd see the orange containers for medicine that I'd seen in films. There was FIJI Water and Starbucks, which seemed fancy. But even something as simple as a brown paper bag felt like a luxury. When you come to the United States, you witness the abundance of products—the sheer amount of food in the grocery store, the cars, and the easy availability of phones. Even with all this overflow of available goods, it was clear that people in America are more valuable than things.

> **WHEN YOU COME TO THE UNITED STATES, YOU WITNESS THE ABUNDANCE OF PRODUCTS—THE SHEER AMOUNT OF FOOD IN THE GROCERY STORE, THE CARS, AND THE EASY AVAILABILITY OF PHONES. EVEN WITH ALL THIS OVERFLOW OF AVAILABLE GOODS, IT WAS CLEAR THAT PEOPLE IN AMERICA ARE MORE VALUABLE THAN THINGS.**

I also quickly discovered the importance of public safety to Americans, which has made me extremely appreciative of the country. Many people think that a person from Russia might move to California because of the weather or the access to venture capitalists in Silicon Valley. Not so—at least not for me. In fact, I've never taken a dime from such money managers.

There are two primary reasons why I moved to the US. First, I sincerely appreciate the uncompromised public safety regulation and the quality of emergency services. In December 2009, a nightclub in Perm, Russia, experienced a deadly fire that changed my view of public safety. This tragedy, known as the Lame Horse fire, happened due to the corruption of inspectors in the city's fire and construction departments.

On the night of the fire, 282 people arrived to celebrate the eighth anniversary of the Lame Horse club. By morning, 156 had died. According to one eyewitness account, only two ambulances came to the site of the fire.[32] When you once lived in a place that didn't have enough emergency vehicles, you feel safe in a different place where you hear sirens.

The second reason is clearly for the entrepreneurial community. I've made my home in Los Angeles. In 2016, I graduated from the UCLA Anderson School and immediately started implementing everything I learned. In 2020, I graduated from Harvard.

All along the way, I've met and partnered with companies that didn't exist in the short time that my business has evolved. Through Xsolla, I've developed great relationships with companies that have dramatically reshaped the video game industry and have built the technologies that have already developed the underlying infrastructure for the Metaverse.

THROUGH XSOLLA, I'VE DEVELOPED GREAT RELATIONSHIPS WITH COMPANIES THAT HAVE DRAMATICALLY RESHAPED THE VIDEO GAME INDUSTRY AND HAVE BUILT THE TECHNOLOGIES THAT HAVE ALREADY DEVELOPED THE UNDERLYING INFRASTRUCTURE FOR THE METAVERSE.

And that's just an appetizer of what is possible in the future.

SCAN ME FOR MORE INFO

CHAPTER 3

WE'RE TALKING TRILLIONS OF DOLLARS HERE, PEOPLE

As a poor student in Siberia, I started my business in 2005 with the goal of purchasing shoes and jeans for myself. Now, nearly twenty years later, Xsolla is an independent technology company helping developers make money in the fast-moving video game sector.

According to Grand View Research, the global video game industry tallied nearly $221 billion in revenue in 2022. Furthermore, the research company estimates that the video game sector will grow at a compound annual growth rate (CAGR) of 12.9 percent through 2030 and reach a total valuation of $584 billion.[33]

I plan to help any brand expand its reach to the Metaverse, which should dwarf the size of the video game industry. This all plays into the ever-growing "Attention Economy." Companies aim to capture and hold customers' attention in today's modern internet. That attention can then be monetized for subscriptions, advertising, and other areas of engagement. As I've noted, Web 2.0 is dominated by large technology companies that use their platforms, influence, and reach. Billions of people visit YouTube,

Twitter, Facebook, and Spotify. These companies collect data, social interactions, personal preferences, and more to monetize each user. But as I'll show you, my vision of the Metaverse will break this centralization and allow anyone to find their audience without relying on these third-party platforms. The Attention Economy will go on . . . but in a much different form.

The early vision of the future Metaverse is found in video games like *Fortnite*, *Apex Legends*, *Minecraft*, *Call of Duty*, and others that offer similar, immersive, interdimensional worlds. For example, *Fortnite* is a game developed by Epic Games that emerged in 2017. While at its heart it is a battle royale game in which players aim to be the last one alive, it is also a massive digital world of unlimited possibilities. In these games, players can enhance their digital avatars, make purchases to advance their characters' strengths and potential, and explore the limits of each map world. Players can also purchase enhancements for their *Fortnite* characters, and even drape them in the fashion brand Balenciaga. In 2021, players could spend upward of $725 for a custom hoodie for their characters and $425 for a plain white T-shirt that reads "Balenciaga: Fortnite."[34] And to be clear, I'm talking about digital clothes for their avatars in the game, not *Fortnite*-branded Balenciaga clothes for the real world.

The possibilities are endless once we extend beyond the gaming sector and begin the process of intersecting our digital worlds with physical ones in all facets. As we move away from the independent worlds of game developers, we'll experience a more enhanced, connected digital system of networks that lets users travel between the digital world and the physical world. And along

I THINK THE METAVERSE SHOULD BE ABOUT PEOPLE EARNING MORE MONEY AND EXPLORING THEIR PASSIONS.

the way, it will be one of the most lucrative periods *ever* for smart, creative people who love to tell their stories and build products.

I have a different vision of the Metaverse and its future than the in-app store vultures at Apple and Amazon. I think the Metaverse should be about people earning more money and exploring their passions. So, I want to explain what the Metaverse means for brands, customers, and creatives. I also want to show you how to stake your claim.

There will be an incredible amount of money available for participants building the Metaverse in the decade ahead. Those who ignore this potential or dismiss it as a fad will find themselves in the same camps as those who failed to embrace the early iterations of the internet, e-commerce, and the digital revolution of mobile applications.

As mentioned earlier, author and Epyllion CEO Matthew Ball projects the Metaverse could reach a value of $30 trillion.[35] That figure would outpace the gross domestic product (GDP) of the United States, the world's largest economy.[36]

I want to take a moment to give you strong evidence for why we are likely closer to the numbers listed above than the far less impressive figures (between $800 billion and $1 trillion) that certain advertising and consulting agencies are touting.[37]

Many individuals have quantified the Metaverse through the gates I mentioned in chapter 1. For example, the total addressable market size linked to AR/VR headsets is roughly one billion users, according to Citi. That would cap the gatekeeping market for AR/ VR at approximately $1 trillion to $2 trillion.[38]

However, this is an incredibly narrow definition. On just the physical front, the whole industry should include the various touchpoints I've discussed: PCs, gaming consoles, smartphones, smartwatches, televisions, and other screens. That expanded ecosystem's hardware alone, Citi notes, could range between $8 trillion and $13 trillion.[39]

But that speaks only to the hardware ecosystem.

What about the trillions of dollars in advertising linked to multichannel efforts that include the Metaverse? What about the in-game purchases, the virtual concert ticket sales, the development of Metasites, and social commerce?

Both at Xsolla and as adherents to the Metaverse and all of its potential, we want to—and ultimately will—quantify the impact of developer and creator economies, dramatic innovation in education, future healthcare ecosystems that bring doctors and patients together, and the role of intelligent manufacturing on the US economy. Over time, the economic activity within the ecosystem will quickly surpass the addressable hardware market. And this is how you can envision a Metaverse that exceeds the value and size of the US economy.

But other things can't be put in dollars and cents. In addition to the monetary potential—the quantitative value of the Metaverse—there will be massive intangible value provided to companies, consumers, and other participants. The improvements to your lifestyle will be at the core of these qualitative intangibles.

Consider that in five to ten years, you will have the opportunity to whisk yourself away to a virtual space anywhere in the world. The Metaverse will provide a "secret door" that you can use to escape from or enhance your physical world.

> CONSIDER THAT IN FIVE TO TEN YEARS, YOU WILL HAVE THE OPPORTUNITY TO WHISK YOURSELF AWAY TO A VIRTUAL SPACE ANYWHERE IN THE WORLD. THE METAVERSE WILL PROVIDE A "SECRET DOOR" THAT YOU CAN USE TO ESCAPE FROM OR ENHANCE YOUR PHYSICAL WORLD.

Tough day at work?

Step into the Metasite of your favorite artist and listen to their music or survey their artwork in a live digital gallery.

Or, instead of driving to a mall, finding parking, pushing through the crowds, trying on various-size clothes, and waiting in line to pay, visit a virtual store. You'll meet with a digital assistant, see the clothing on your virtual avatar, and instantly settle payment for the products you want in your size. Within two days, you'll receive them via delivery to your home. Those are just two examples of how the Metaverse will bring real intangible value to your life. It will save you time. It will save you money.

I'm incredibly excited about the potential of the Metaverse for education. There was a time when students had to visit libraries, find research papers and books, cite them by hand, and type long research papers on typewriters (without spell-check). Today, a research paper can be written in far less time from the comfort of anywhere, thanks to the current infrastructure of the internet and software enhancements.

In the future Metaverse, students will virtually visit historical sites and events. They will use artificial intelligence to better craft papers and expand their knowledge and storytelling abilities. These technological advancements provide utility to your life, and you can't put a price on how they will enhance your lifestyle.

To understand the potential of the Metaverse, we must also take a step back and understand the technological changes that have occurred in recent decades.

The advancement of technology will not only expand the potential of today's Metaverse. It will also fuel a period of economic and technological growth that makes things possible that we have yet to conceive. For years, we've witnessed changes in our lives through the invention of digital commerce, networking systems, remote workplace connectivity, fiber-optic networks, and advanced online speeds.

The Metaverse will rely on faster networks, robust cyber-security protocols, more potent graphics cards, and other enhancements to reach its potential. Some of that technology exists today, while other components must be further developed.

As this technology reaches commercial and industrial capacity, it will quickly reshape our lives, drive down costs, and bring us all closer together. As these technological leaps unfold in the years ahead, consumers and companies must understand their role in early adoption.

INTEROPERABILITY IS KEY

When I started my company, online and mobile video gaming was essentially free. Consumers would play games, and roughly 10 percent would pay for in-game upgrades or bonuses. I quickly realized that improving the system that facilitated payments could help improve the number of people participating in these purchases. Bringing that 10 percent threshold to 20 percent simply by making it easier for consumers to make in-app purchases helped increase profitability immensely for developers. It offered them even more opportunities to develop their games, create new iterations, and accelerate their potential. By providing the tools for payments across different networks, game developers will have incentives to not only improve their gaming but also identify new ways to maximize their add-ons and reasons for consumers to keep playing and buying in the game.

Look at the most successful games of the last decade. Most Americans will know *Candy Crush Saga*, *FarmVille*, and even *Kim Kardashian: Hollywood*. These games have extremely loyal followings, generate lots of revenue, and create unique challenges that many consumers will gladly pay to bypass. Want to skip a level? Games will now allow you to do so for a premium thanks to the underlying payment systems that enable these level advancements and bonus tools to exist. Those in-game purchases are what non-gamers typically think of when they consider mobile game spending—and they might believe such payments will be gateways in the future of the Metaverse.

I want to dispel the myth that spending in the Metaverse will look anything like skipping Level 38 in *Jelly Splash* or a similar mobile game. In the Metaverse, consumer spending—and the motivations behind that spending—will take on a new definition. No longer will consumers pay to bypass levels. Instead, their spending will center on enhancing their interdimensional experiences between the real and virtual worlds, and it will all come down to one critical word that defines the consumer experience in the Metaverse: *interoperability*.

Interoperability refers to a very specific set of skills.

No, not like Liam Neeson's very specific skills in the movie *Taken*.

I'm talking about specific skills and technical abilities of VR or AR platforms. These abilities will allow users to travel between physical and virtual worlds. In their travels, they won't experience any disruption to their experience. They won't face any roadblocks when trying to bring their digital wallets that include payment tools, digital items, and more. Users should not be forced to use a certain payment system in one digital world and a different system in another world. Think of a place where you aren't constrained by the type of credit card you carry when trying to pay at a restaurant. By default, interoperability prevents more prominent brands from cornering a specific technology or platform. It ensures that there are no physical moats between digital worlds.

Interoperability is critical to the user experience. It must be seamless. Only then can it allow humans to interact with the virtual content and experiences at the heart of this $30 trillion movement. Interoperability means users can take virtual goods (purchased in the Metaverse) from one system or world to the next. It means they can communicate with other users across all virtual and real-world environments—without interruption—regardless of whether they are using virtual reality headsets, desktop computer chats, or any other hardware of their choice. No interruption.

Think of it this way.

There are no *real* physical assets in the Metaverse.

A Gucci sweater or a pair of Adidas shoes in the Metaverse are not real in physical terms. They are just lines of code resulting in an image of the sweater or the basketball shoes, stored within large computing networks. These lines of code must communicate with networks and systems. This communication is what allows a user to take their digital assets across the Metaverse—thus enhancing the value of these assets and increasing the user reach. Consumers want to make one purchase and bring that product and style everywhere. These items must not only be allowed to be purchased but should also be allowed to be traded.

Those technologies are critical in communication. They're also essential in how users present themselves, their values, their goals, and their interests. Expressing these things is crucial in the real world, and it will be crucial in the virtual world. That expression tells others who we are and what matters to us—wherever we are and however we are interacting with other people.

The following five elements will define the user experience in the future and largely reflect how users will spend money on brands, products, and services in the Metaverse. Specifically, I want to highlight

1. personal expression
2. social interaction
3. accessible community
4. immersive education
5. personalized entertainment

First is *personal expression*. At its core, the Metaverse provides users with a means of expressing themselves like never before. Their ability to create a digital identity—constructed in the images and brands of their choice—is both meaningful and unrivaled in terms of previous social interactions. Users will be able to express different parts of their identity in ways that may not be possible in the physical world—whether it's due to economic, political, or social forces. Consumers may value the opportunity to create and customize their avatars, clothing, and other virtual assets as a form of self-expression.

Second, personal expression will enhance *social interaction* as customers in the Metaverse will have unprecedented choices in brands and the ability to express their values through purchases, the worlds they explore, and the relationships they build. The ability to express oneself in this environment will enable meaningful connections with other users, expanding people's capacity to make new friends and to find others who share their interests and styles.

Third, an *accessible community* will enable users to find a place where they belong. The Metaverse will give individuals access to sites, products, ideas, and communities that they may not be able to obtain in the physical world—again, for reasons that could be economic, political, or social. A sense of community gives people a shared system of values and allows them to participate in activities with like-minded individuals.

The community can provide and enhance my final two key consumer pillars of the Metaverse. Individuals may wish to find independence and interest in the remaining areas. The beauty is, in the Metaverse, they can collaborate with the community or seek independent opportunities in the fourth and fifth elements, *immersive education* and *personalized entertainment*.

As I noted, the internet was a great equalizer for me personally. I obtained a business and entrepreneurial education for free by learning from countless sources online. There were YouTube videos, digital libraries, how-to blogs, and content that focused explicitly on the skills I needed to build a digital network.

The Metaverse will take education to the next level, providing incredible, immersive tools for anyone to develop new skills, participate in virtual training, enlist in educational programs, take lectures from anywhere in the world (or even in deep space), and explore concepts new and foreign to them.

THE METAVERSE WILL TAKE EDUCATION TO THE NEXT LEVEL, PROVIDING INCREDIBLE, IMMERSIVE TOOLS FOR ANYONE TO DEVELOP NEW SKILLS, PARTICIPATE IN VIRTUAL TRAINING, ENLIST IN EDUCATIONAL PROGRAMS, TAKE LECTURES FROM ANYWHERE IN THE WORLD (OR EVEN IN DEEP SPACE), AND EXPLORE CONCEPTS NEW AND FOREIGN TO THEM.

Of course, everything can't be all work. Entertainment is the last pillar that I'll discuss. The Metaverse will provide the most significant source of entertainment in the history of technology. It will give individuals incalculable opportunities to explore the digital and physical worlds, interact with creative minds, play games, attend sports events and live concerts, or challenge their friends on the other side of the globe to contests. When I say the limits don't exist, it's because they will not.

If you think you're good enough to challenge a digital version of chess grandmaster Boris Spassky or Bobby Fischer to a match in Manhattan's Washington Square Park, you'll have that chance. White pieces or black pieces? You'll make that call.

The transition between the virtual and physical worlds will initially seem foreign to many brand managers. There will be fundamental changes to the study and practice of branding itself. Remember that virtual worlds will alter how people see and perceive brands, heightening the social importance of products and services through consumer interactions. In many ways, brand managers will need to go back to school or reimagine branding in this new context.

If you're a brand manager, you should know the two key elements a company's brand must provide its customers: trust and self-expression. This is taught at every business school.

At the core of the brand and consumer dynamic is a relationship built on *trust*. Trust is an intangible value that establishes the customer's beliefs about a brand's credibility, quality, and personal meaning. If a product has an excellent reputation, consumers expect the company will guarantee its products, replace defective ones, provide excellent customer service, and maintain its reputation and product quality.

But in the digital world, products shouldn't be defective unless there is a fundamental problem with the computer code supporting it. An avatar's shirt won't get holes in it, and there won't be people calling customer service to say that a digital pair of sneakers don't fit correctly. Therefore, the second element of a brand's intangible value and quality—*self-expression*—will be tested even more. People want to signal to others what the brand means to them. It signals that the products are excellent and that those who use or wear them are wealthy, muscular, cool, athletic, or whatever other associations the customer sees in the brand. In many ways, customers will define the value of the brand.

Some brands even go beyond their core audience. For example, skateboarding brands like Supreme, Palace, and A BATHING APE have developed cult followings over the decades. In addition to their core audience, they've been able to gain incredible popularity among people who've never even stepped on a skateboard. Why do those people purchase goods from these brands? Perhaps because they want to associate themselves with skateboarders and the skateboard culture, or present to the world that they are "cool."

Self-expression—and the customers who subsequently express the values of the brand as part of their identity—will be a vital component of the Metaverse. This positioning of self-expression is a radical shift for the meaning of brands. Over the next few years, companies will ask themselves an essential series of questions, including, *What does our brand mean today, and what will it mean in the future?* But brand managers must also ask what their *customers* believe the brand means and what values it portrays.

This is important because brands will evolve in the Metaverse. The company's brand will reflect individually on a customer's core values, economic status, and even social perspectives. The onset of the Metaverse is already testing the authenticity of brands like Burberry, Nike, and Tiffany & Co.—all early adopters of the Metaverse. We are about to experience a dramatic shift in the definition of branding and how brand experiences alter relationships between company and customer.

What opportunities will exist to enhance a brand and discover customer views?

First, let's focus on virtual brand experiences. These will help companies identify new customers and create new points of interaction outside the real world that were previously impossible. For example, a photographer or painter might put on a virtual art show in a San Francisco art gallery featuring a view of the Golden Gate Bridge. A timeshare company might give virtual tours of properties overlooking the mountains. A travel agent might take prospective customers on a tour of places they could visit across the continents. A car dealership might allow virtual test drives of new or used models. An interior designer and construction team might show an aspiring restaurant owner several designs of what the bar might look like—from inside a virtual version of the space—before a single brick is laid or a nail is hammered. These virtual brand experiences will help companies start their brand testing in the Metaverse, enable constructive feedback, and, of course, sell to willing customers.

Over time, they will help companies answer those critical questions of what their brands mean to customers, what customers value, and how virtual experiences shape the perception of their products in the real world. For example, virtual experiences may be critical for companies trying to expand into new product categories or improve their reputation for quality in physical products. These virtual brand experiences can be vital make-or-break moments for customer acquisition. They might also present a breakthrough that helps bring a new generation of customers to their products.

Second, any company that isn't building its virtual storefronts now will pay an exorbitant cost in the future when the infrastructure is more expensive. Metasites will enable customers to explore new products and purchase items. Imagine a more immersive sales experience that brings customers directly to a company's door. I will explain the value of these Metasites in a later chapter. For now, think of them as an opportunity to build a store on Fifth Avenue in Manhattan . . . without the costs of the physical storefront. These Metasites will be completely customizable, allowing a brand to directly reflect its values and its style to the customer. In addition, they can serve as unrivaled revenue centers.

Third, if you thought Instagram influencers were a big financial success over the last decade, just wait; the Metaverse will take influencer marketing to the next level. Brands will partner with virtual influencers in the Metaverse to attract eyeballs to products and services. Virtual events will present opportunities for exclusive products and experiences.

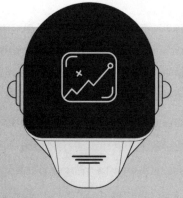

IF YOU THOUGHT INSTAGRAM INFLUENCERS WERE A BIG FINANCIAL SUCCESS OVER THE LAST DECADE, JUST WAIT; THE METAVERSE WILL TAKE INFLUENCER MARKETING TO THE NEXT LEVEL.

Today, 61 percent of all customers trust influencer marketing on social media sites and other platforms, according to Shopify.[40] While the influencer marketing world was valued at only $16.4 billion in 2022, based on my estimation, the Metaverse has the potential to easily drive that market north of $100 billion given the untapped potential of that advertising economy.[41] The influencer marketing industry is still in its infancy, and the advent of Metasites will create incredible opportunities for public speakers, celebrities, and others to endorse products.

Finally, sponsorship opportunities will also explode in the Metaverse. Brands will compete for in-game-style advertising space at virtual events like concerts. Remember the virtual art show in San Francisco that I mentioned earlier? Imagine the possibilities of advertising and marketing that come along with these live events—and the opportunities to bundle products with other brands.

These opportunities will promote brand awareness and help direct traffic directly to a company's Metasite. During a virtual event, a customer can quickly jump over to another company's

Metasite to learn about its product or service and then seamlessly jump back into the previous experience without interruption (even if that event is the Super Bowl). That is what the technology and range of the Metaverse will offer in the decade ahead.

The Metaverse will provide opportunities for brands to connect with consumers and build brand awareness like nothing before. As this Metaverse evolves, more opportunities will emerge, offering incredible potential for developers, storytellers, brand managers, and independent minds to expand their creativity.

I'm especially excited about the Metaverse because of the opportunity ahead for content creators. I'm thrilled to see what independent creators can do as they build on existing technologies, establish new brands, and tell their stories. It's all about the potential for creative expression and the chance to make real money. As we move away from traditional, centralized platforms like Google Play, Amazon Music, or Apple Music—where millions of views can lead to minuscule financial rewards—creatives will make even more money on royalties, strategic partnerships, and other projects. Content creators can directly monetize their work through several methods.

Let's explore the primary opportunities.

At the core sits the Metasites, which, again, I'll discuss in depth in chapter 6. This digital real estate is a critical commodity that will allow creators to sell virtual experiences and items for consumers to own or interact with. Want to put on a digital concert? Want to hang your art on the wall in a physical space? Want to host a booth at a digital theme park or a stadium during a major event? These virtual Metaverse spaces will help you achieve real sales, boost your royalties, and engage with global consumers. Metasites will be incredibly valuable for authors, actors, playwrights, film producers, artists, social influencers, YouTube personalities, and anyone else with a story. They will act as the anchor to a small business's brand and attract attention from around the world.

The second significant opportunity ahead that will help you make real money is through the sale of non-fungible tokens (NFTs). NFTs are unique digital assets that guarantee the exclusive ownership of a virtual item or experience.

NFTs create immediate scarcity and incredible brand potential for sales and unique products. Since they are tracked on a blockchain, these assets cannot be stolen, hacked, or compromised. (We will discuss the blockchain in chapter 7.) Additionally, they cannot be counterfeited given the strict authentication processes on the blockchain. If only one version of something exists, its scarcity value can rise significantly, and interoperability allows the owner to showcase that exclusive product across the digital and real worlds. The tools that exist to ensure such authenticity and originality include reverse image searches, blockchain explorers, and digital authenticity certificates.

A common question people ask when discussing NFTs centers on security: "Can NFTs be counterfeited?"

The simple answer is no. NFTs are unique assets tracked on blockchain technology. Blockchain makes it possible to verify owners and the authenticity or exclusivity of the asset. When stored on the blockchain, one can see the unique identification verifications.

On the blockchain, we can see the official record of ownership and transfer history. This cannot be altered. Once the NFT is established on the blockchain, its authenticity cannot be challenged. To counterfeit an NFT would mean someone altered the verification documentation on the blockchain. Should someone try to copy an NFT, it would lack the verification identification.

That said, artwork and collectibles could technically be copied or counterfeited. However, the NFT's value comes from its uniqueness and its ability to verify authenticity on the blockchain. Now, it's worth noting that between 2020 and 2021, there was a real valuation bubble of NFTs and other digital assets. It's important to note that in the history of finance, there are traditionally waves of speculation around a new technology or real estate. The Metaverse is no exception to the phenomenon. The good news is that this cycle created awareness of these future technologies and established the early pipelines for development among content creators. NFTs will be a vital part of the future of e-commerce and the success of the Metaverse's ecosystem.

Already, major brands are getting into the NFT space, including sports organizations like the National Football League and Major League Baseball, athletic companies like Nike and lululemon, and countless others. The value of the global NFT market stands to reach at least $211.72 billion by 2030, according to Grand View Research.[42] However, Emergen Research said in June 2022 that the global market could reach $3.5 trillion by 2030, depending on economic conditions.[43]

Finally, for content creators, the best opportunity to make money, at the risk of sounding self-serving, is through Metasites and consumer-facing transactions. It's simple: you can capitalize on in-app purchases and microtransactions as customers look to enhance their experiences in the Metaverse. These purchases will be on virtual items they can take between the virtual and physical worlds. There will be an entire subindustry of hypercustomization when it comes to avatars and personalization to each individual user.

These purchases include clothing, skins, stickers, and other accessories for virtual avatars. They include add-ons for virtual concerts or exclusive events inside the Metaverse. These in-app transactions will provide steady streams of royalties for content creators and brands alike.

These three payment categories (X, Y, and Z) exist right now—on the back of traditional financial systems. In the future, the Metaverse will evolve and expand. This will likely create new opportunities for advertising, brand building, creative partnerships, and even consulting. The more this virtual world grows, the bigger the pie for early adopters. And it's a reminder that creatives will run this world—not the traditional financiers who have dominated the real one for centuries.

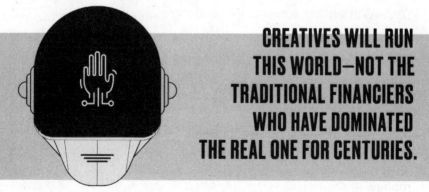

CREATIVES WILL RUN THIS WORLD—NOT THE TRADITIONAL FINANCIERS WHO HAVE DOMINATED THE REAL ONE FOR CENTURIES.

A MESSAGE TO WALL STREET, BANKS, AND SILICON VALLEY

Much like the real world, the Metaverse won't be created by Wall Street financial institutions like Goldman Sachs or J.P. Morgan, central banks like the Federal Reserve or the Bank of England, or centralized players like Meta Platforms or Apple. While all these entities aim to push influence on the Metaverse, content creators and businesses will be the ones to build it from the ground up.

That's how the world's largest economy evolved in the United States—one small business and one consumer at a time. In simple terms, small businesses in America employ more than half of the workers, and consumers are responsible for more than 70 percent of GDP spending.[44] I expect that the Metaverse will evolve and replicate these metrics. This is how human nature and capitalism operate. And it will be an incredible feat to witness.

Meanwhile, the central players in the current iteration of the internet and e-commerce—like Amazon, Apple's App Store, and Alphabet—largely don't make money on their own products; they do so by aggregating and selling products created by others. For example, in the third quarter of 2022, 58 percent of products sold on Amazon's e-commerce platform were sold by third parties.[45] These platforms are massive economic engines.

Naturally, these players have a lot to lose, not only in sales potential but also over influence in the potential economy. In the Metaverse, companies like Google and Apple—which act as intermediaries for financial transactions—will no longer be required. Blockchain and cryptocurrencies will enable a seamless payment system that ends the feudalistic nature of the internet for users.

Instead of Google and Apple sucking up money in their app stores, that money can go directly to the businesses and the creators.

Over time, the hundreds of billions, and eventually trillions, of dollars generated by the Metaverse can be allocated to new user acquisitions, advertising, and new projects that expand a brand's life cycle.

DON'T GET LEFT BEHIND

I see incredible opportunities in the Metaverse, decentralized platforms, and Web3.

My company Xsolla operates in a business-to-consumer industry. We live inside the video gaming space for *Fortnite* and other games. Our clients include large developers and independent producers who are just getting started. We've helped aggregate games and payment options in a business model that will be successful in the long term. Now, we want to show everyone the potential of what lies ahead for the Metaverse. We can move away from the centralized players that nickel-and-dime content producers across multiple industries.

Every time people use payment services outside of the major game-specific digital storefronts, they come to us to engage consumers through microtransactions. This helps in-game developers make more money, enables consumers to use the games they want, and cuts out the intermediaries in the system.

My goal is to make Xsolla a business engine that transforms the future of content creation and gives anyone with a simple beginning like mine access to a world of customers. We are increasingly working with creative brands, content producers, and others who want to stake their claim in the Metaverse.

Trillions of dollars will be up for grabs as content creators take it all back . . . and deservedly so. The days of earning millions of views on YouTube or other mega platforms and receiving pennies on the dollar are numbered—which is why those platforms are shaking in their virtual boots.

In my opinion, as they should be.

THE DAYS OF EARNING MILLIONS OF VIEWS ON YOUTUBE OR OTHER MEGA PLATFORMS AND RECEIVING PENNIES ON THE DOLLAR ARE NUMBERED— WHICH IS WHY THOSE PLATFORMS ARE SHAKING IN THEIR VIRTUAL BOOTS.

SCAN ME FOR MORE INFO

THE COLLAPSE OF THE MOVIE, MUSIC, AND BOOK INDUSTRIES AND THE RISE OF THE VIDEO GAME

I've spent my life in awe of content creators.

From the storytellers behind video games to the producers and directors behind films (and, of course, the actors featured in them). From the musicians who pour their hearts into songs and compositions to the writers who draft incredible fiction and nonfiction. Since I was a teenager in Russia, I've viewed creative content as a window to a better world.

THE COMPENSATION GULF IN CREATIVE INDUSTRIES

The creative spirit is as rich as ever, with countless streaming channels for film and music offering more choices and revenue potential. As a result, consumers now buy more books, listen to more music, and watch more television and films than ever before.

And they're doing so on even more devices—phones, tablets, computers, and now, even watches.

So, why does it sometimes feel like these industries are failing?

Why is adequate compensation for creatives still such a struggle? As I'll later explain in more depth, current royalty structures benefit large production studios and entertainment platforms, while artists traditionally receive a pittance of the total revenue generated.

And why do just a few significant entities hold so much economic and legal power?

Today, creators are poorly compensated for their efforts and lack collaboration tools to maximize revenue from their most passionate fans. Musicians, filmmakers, authors, and other creatives are bound to an antiquated royalty payment system that fails to incentivize new projects and a new content model that puts the focus on user growth rather than revenue maximization. The current payment system also fails to let creators properly plan and execute new projects or maximize interaction with their best customers.

The good news is that things will change when the Metaverse reaches its full potential. It's critical to educate creators on increasing revenue, personal data ownership, and audience engagement. There are trillions of dollars up for grabs, starting right now.

Before I share the most significant reason behind under-whelming compensation today, we'll look at the root cause of why creative compensation has collapsed over the last twenty years. We'll explore the past, present, and future of creative compensation. Then, we'll explore why the video game industry revenue dwarfs the size of the film, music, and publishing industries combined. As the Metaverse expands—bringing digital tools and products for creatives to the forefront—these three industries can unleash best practices that hopefully, one day, retire the phrase "starving artist."

HOW CREATIVES ARE PAID NOW

Today, content creators are largely compensated through royalty payments. Royalties are typically paid as a percentage of the total sales for each published work (film, music, book, etc.) over a period. Creatives may also receive a fixed compensation amount for each use of their work, depending on the contract. These payments are commonly paid by an organization that is using the work. These payers include record labels, publishers, and film studios. In addition, payments can be sent to royalty collection agencies, which mediate between creatives and their customers (users). These agencies also work on artists' behalf to negotiate royalty payments, which have grown more complex in the last twenty years. Challenges date back much further, well before the Copyright Act of 1978 that altered the timetables for copyright durations.

In the music sector, there are various types of royalty payments. Artists and songwriters may receive royalty payments after the sale of their music. Examples include a percentage for each sale of an album, each download from a digital distributor, or every thousand plays on a streaming service. Musicians may also receive royalties for use of their work in other channels. For example, they may

IT'S CRITICAL TO EDUCATE CREATORS ON INCREASING REVENUE, PERSONAL DATA OWNERSHIP, AND AUDIENCE ENGAGEMENT.

receive royalties every time a song is played in a film, in a TV show, or during live events like football or baseball games.

This system is complex. Self-published authors will receive a percentage of the number of books sold or for every download through a digital distributor like Amazon's Kindle. In the traditional publishing industry, authors receive an up-front payment (or advance). After publication, publishers draw down royalty payments until book sales exceed the advance. In most cases, an author never sees another dollar for their book.

Meanwhile, journalists have quickly flocked to Substack, an independent publishing platform that removes the centralized nature of reporting and pays writers above market rate for their perspective. Substack allows writers to build their own personal audiences who pay a subscription—typically $5 to $10 per month— for exclusive content.

Film royalties are also straightforward. Actors and screenwriters may receive royalties every time a DVD or digital version of a film is purchased or when a movie is shown in theaters. They may also receive a royalty payment when their film is shown on network cable.

A PRIMER ON THE ROYALTY SYSTEM

Now, if you're new to this payment system, let's take a step back. Royalty payments in the music industry date back to the early twentieth century—which is why I call the modern version an *antiquated* practice. At the time, the US government began to debate the concept of intellectual property rights and how they applied to the music industry. Before royalty systems emerged, musicians and composers were paid a one-time fee for creating their work. They had no control over how other companies and users engaged with their work and received no further compensation for commercial use.

The industry changed with the introduction of performing rights organizations (PROs). These companies began to lobby for the financial interest of songwriters and composers. Today, the three primary PROs are ASCAP (American Society of Composers, Authors, and Publishers), BMI (Broadcast Music, Inc.), and SESAC (Society of European Stage Authors and Composers).

These entities collect royalty payments from groups that use music publicly. This can include compensation for song use on broadcasts like YouTube or FM radio or from live concerts or performances. The PROs then distribute those payments to the musicians and songwriters.

There are two forms of music copyrights—master and publishing. Master rights are provided to the music's owners. This can include a musician, copywriter, studio, or individuals who fund the recording. Publishing rights refer to the song's composer and consist of the lyrics, melodies, and other production.

Why does this distinction matter? It allows a musician the opportunity to receive payments two times when the song is played, depending on their agreement and role in the content's creation. They can also make money when other musicians play or perform their songs.

For decades, musicians collected royalties as payment for the sale of vinyl records, CDs, tapes, and physical forms of music. The industry dramatically changed in the late 1990s with the advancement of the internet. Napster, a digital file-sharing site, made the distribution of music across the internet easy and sparked an explosion in the practice of *freebooting*.

This term refers to the unauthorized use and distribution of copyrighted works. Users could download music on Napster and then burn the songs onto a CD or put them on an MP3 device, all without any compensation going to the creators and studios. The service was popular with consumers, who could illegally access music for free (and often without consequence). However, this practice represented a significant source of lost revenue for musicians and studios, setting off major court battles and changes to royalty practices.

Music industry officials and artists recognized that the rise of streaming would eviscerate their existing business model, which relied on selling physical products like CDs and vinyl records. This theory proved correct. Revenue plunged.

With the rise of streaming, the industry needed to understand how to monetize music better and ensure that artists received compensation for digital downloads and sharing. This helped fuel the rise of music streaming services like Apple Music, Spotify, and Amazon Music, which act as centralized hubs for content distribution.

While the government moved to make unauthorized streaming illegal, the effort to centralize music put artists and content creators in a new financial pinch. Despite a rise in consumption through streaming, royalty payments for the vast number of artists declined on the aggregate. Today, musicians receive payment on the number of times a song is played, streamed, or downloaded and far less on the physical products of the previous decades.

WITH THE RISE OF STREAMING, THE INDUSTRY NEEDED TO UNDERSTAND HOW TO MONETIZE MUSIC BETTER AND ENSURE THAT ARTISTS RECEIVED COMPENSATION FOR DIGITAL DOWNLOADS AND SHARING. THIS HELPED FUEL THE RISE OF MUSIC STREAMING SERVICES LIKE APPLE MUSIC, SPOTIFY, AND AMAZON MUSIC, WHICH ACT AS CENTRALIZED HUBS FOR CONTENT DISTRIBUTION.

The massive shift toward digital streaming has altered the way musicians receive payments and fueled the online distribution of music through the digital service providers (DSPs) listed above.

Today, these DSPs will distribute royalties to the rights holders while the PROs continue to fight for better royalty terms. Unfortunately, the current system has a wide variety of flaws. A lack of transparency in both physical and streaming numbers has made it very difficult for creators to track and confirm the usage of their works. As a result, it is challenging for creatives to know how much money they should receive. This has also fueled lawsuits between musicians and management.

For example, in 2018, singer and songwriter Melissa Etheridge sued her management, alleging underpayment of royalties. Etheridge's lawsuit is just one example of a case primarily fueled by confusion around the outdated and complex payment systems that have become the norm of the last century.

The shift toward digital music and film has also fueled a decline in royalty rates, with payment delays becoming more common. This is incredibly frustrating to artists, as they not only feel that they can't properly track the money owed to them but they also recognize that the digital transition has decreased the value of intellectual property.

Finally, the shift toward these powerful DSPs, like Apple Music, has drastically reduced the market power of the artists. The existing contracts in the space are heavily in favor of those large players. Apple can now engage in marketing wars to gain more consumers and engineer an even smaller amount of money that artists believe they are entitled to in their business.

Today, negotiating royalty rates is time-consuming and nearly impossible for creators just starting in the business. Most lack the resources to maximize their revenue and largely feel that they must take what is given to them under the service agreements of these DSPs.

What's incredible about this digital transition is how greatly it financially impacted the overall revenue of the movie, music, and book publishing industries. In 1999, music sales, on an inflation-adjusted level, peaked at $23.7 billion, according to Statista. The industry's recorded music revenue cratered to $7.7 billion in 2014 and steadily recovered to $14.9 billion in 2021.[46]

According to the Recording Industry Association of America (RIAA), in 2021, ad-supported and subscription-based music combined represented 83 percent of the music industry's revenue.[47] Again, this was all positive for the consumer but terrible for content creators.

Meanwhile, in the film industry, inflation-adjusted spending at the box office peaked in 2002 at $14.5 billion, with the average price of a ticket that year at $5.81, according to tracking site The Numbers.[48] Before COVID-19 hit the US film industry, inflation-adjusted box office sales totaled just $12.8 billion in 2019. The average ticket price that year was $9.16, nearly 57.6 percent higher than a ticket at the start of the century.[49]

More than ever, movie theaters rely on a handful of blockbuster films or a significant amount of Hollywood reboots to keep them in operation. They might also rely on studios that specialize in niche genres like horror, despite the fact that most horror films are cheaply made and forgettable. Yet, keep in mind, movie theaters make the bulk of their money from their concession stands.

Box office attendance has collapsed, creating even greater pressure on filmmakers to embrace the digital transition toward streaming. Unfortunately, this industry has yet to fully understand the potential revenue generation possible from existing technologies and customer spending patterns.

This is the "state of play" for the entertainment industry. So why is the "state of playing"—the video gaming industry—valued at nearly $200 billion today?[50] That's right, it's worth more than the film, music, and book publishing industries *combined*.

By 2026, the video gaming sector could reach $321 billion in revenue, according to consulting giant PwC and data collected by the World Economic Forum.[51]

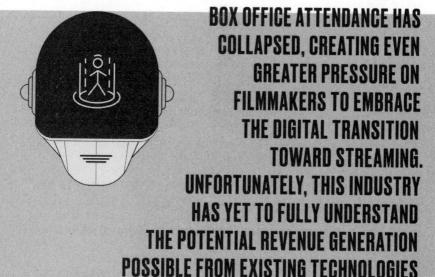

BOX OFFICE ATTENDANCE HAS COLLAPSED, CREATING EVEN GREATER PRESSURE ON FILMMAKERS TO EMBRACE THE DIGITAL TRANSITION TOWARD STREAMING. UNFORTUNATELY, THIS INDUSTRY HAS YET TO FULLY UNDERSTAND THE POTENTIAL REVENUE GENERATION POSSIBLE FROM EXISTING TECHNOLOGIES AND CUSTOMER SPENDING PATTERNS.

So how is it that this sector—which so many people dismiss and/or whose financials they never take the time to study—is growing at an exceptional pace and will continue to dwarf the revenue generated by legacy entertainment sectors?

HOW VIDEO GAMES MONETIZE DIFFERENTLY

It's not as if video game companies have a magical additional revenue stream or technology that isn't available to other sectors. Video game companies make money through advertising revenue, sponsored content, and brand partnerships.

They monetize on subscription-based platforms like Twitch and receive royalty payments for their products. They sell merchandise like shirts and hats that feature the brands. They can obtain capital through donation platforms like Kickstarter and sell games through digital platforms like Apple's App Store. Music studios, film studios, and artists all do the same thing.

But in addition to the growing revenue streams and digital platforms at the industry's backbone, video gaming embraces one of the most important economic forces in the world—the 80/20 principle.

Video game developers understand that the key source of their revenue derives from a small group of users. According to Newzoo, there are roughly 3.2 billion video game consumers.[52] I estimate that roughly 80 percent of revenue comes from only 20 percent of the users. The largest fraction of revenue derives from a group of players I call *whales*.

Just like the casinos of Las Vegas, the whales make content creators the most money. For example, there are users of gaming platforms who pay nothing, or close to nothing, and there are people who are not willing to pay for digital goods at all because they do not interpret digital goods as an actual purchase. Other users might spend $100 to $200 per month on these games with in-app purchases or digital enhancements. But on the extreme level—the whale level—some users will pay upward of $10,000 per month.

Or look at the music industry. In August 2023, the music-streaming platform Spotify had 551 million monthly users, of which 220 million were paid subscribers. So, 331 million people, or about 60 percent, listened to the ad-generated music for free, while about 39 percent paid to subscribe.[53] That is the business model, and users can listen to as little or as much music as they want on the subscription platform. There aren't major efforts by streaming companies to engage the superusers of music to maximize revenue.

From the consumer perspective, these platforms are great for their choice and budget. However, Apple Music and Spotify compete, usually with extended free trials or competitive pricing that pushes the value of music lower and lower. Things became so difficult for musicians that international superstar Taylor Swift called out Apple CEO Tim Cook for acknowledging the pressure these price battles have on the artists selling or streaming music on the platforms.[54] Not only did these streaming platforms engage in trial periods that made revenue generation more challenging, but they also began marketing practices like bundling for family subscriptions. These practices drive down revenue for the industry.

I believe these services fail to make money—and benefit content producers—because they don't maximize enough revenue potential from superusers, the people willing to spend more than $10 per month on a subscription. A few companies have tried to grasp this concept—but only around the edges. For example, the streaming service TIDAL does offer a separate $20 subscription tier that provides direct payments to musicians and artists. I think the industry has the potential to do far better.

Through the right incentives, partnerships, and product development, the superusers could generate $100 per month or more, helping musicians and other creatives maximize their revenue.

This challenge isn't limited to the music business. I have discussed music more than film because that industry has generated more controversy around royalty payments than others in recent years. However, the explosion of subscribers to digital streaming services like Netflix and Hulu has created similar price pressures on film and TV creators.

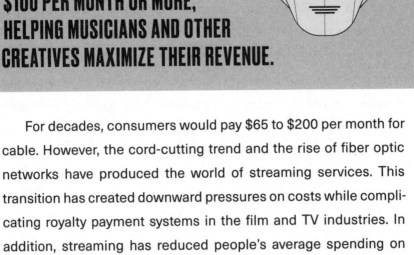

THROUGH THE RIGHT INCENTIVES, PARTNERSHIPS, AND PRODUCT DEVELOPMENT, THE SUPERUSERS COULD GENERATE $100 PER MONTH OR MORE, HELPING MUSICIANS AND OTHER CREATIVES MAXIMIZE THEIR REVENUE.

For decades, consumers would pay $65 to $200 per month for cable. However, the cord-cutting trend and the rise of fiber optic networks have produced the world of streaming services. This transition has created downward pressures on costs while complicating royalty payment systems in the film and TV industries. In addition, streaming has reduced people's average spending on in-home entertainment, negatively impacting the advertising industry. And while these services do benefit consumers, this shift to streaming isn't good for the creators.

In today's streaming wars, companies continue to engage in long-winded "free trial" battles, attempt to force exclusivity onto creative producers, and fail to maximize revenue. For example, Netflix has about 238 million paid subscribers worldwide who pay different monthly amounts for the service, depending on the streaming quality, the number of screens they use, and their country market (among other factors).[55]

This subscription model has essentially forced creators into a work-for-hire agreement in which they receive a fixed amount of capital for their projects and small royalty payments when the product is consumed. And with more competition building, content wars will likely accelerate.

Yet Netflix hasn't embraced the 80/20 principle—the idea that it could generate far more revenue from a select number of participants (its whales) who might be willing to pay a larger amount of money for special features to shows, expanded or bonus content, or access to early releases.

In addition, there have been moves by Disney+ and other services to derive money from the pre-release of a film that aligns with the cost of seeing a box-office film in the theaters. But I still argue that superusers can generate far more money, based on my experience and knowledge of the video gaming industry.

I have long wondered why film studios do not attempt to maximize their audiences through special theatrical release events or bonus content for superusers of a franchise. Today, musicians can command hundreds of dollars for a concert, but film studios still rely on the universal population for economic support. Imagine if movie franchises with very defined and committed audiences—like *Star Wars*, *Star Trek*, and the Marvel Cinematic Universe—offered special access to a film or bonus content one month ahead of a broader release.

Based on what we have seen in the superuser base for the video gaming industry, these whales could provide an incredible boost in revenue to content producers. A ticket to a special release party could generate hundreds of dollars, just like concerts and sporting events.

These are easy methods that can improve the top-line revenue in these industries. Users are spending less and less on entertainment, even in the face of greater proliferation across all sectors. Companies are just scratching the surface of how to maximize revenue from their superusers.

In 2013, Daft Punk released *Random Access Memories*—one of my favorite albums and their best. Prior to the official release date, they sold an early version of the album on Apple Music. As a big fan of Daft Punk, I listened to the album two weeks before everyone else and paid less than $20 to do so.

There was potential to increase spending from a Daft Punk fan like me during that period before the album became widely available on streaming platforms. Whatever they might have offered during those two weeks, I would have happily paid for! And so would millions of other Daft Punk fans. Such opportunities are not only great for the avid fans who are willing to pay for them but can also maximize revenue on behalf of the artists.

ENGAGEMENT IS KING

With today's technology, so much more is possible for these industries. The way I envision the maximization of revenue among whales is simple. Let's say we're watching a television show together, like HBO's hit *Game of Thrones*. While one of us gets up to make popcorn, we pause the show and a screen with a QR code appears. When I scan the code, I am taken directly to a store where I can purchase physical products like T-shirts, digital items like sticker pages for Instagram, or interoperable objects that an avatar may wear in the Metaverse. These simple products might sell for as little as $2.99. Just like that, a new revenue stream is born, even before the popcorn is ready!

Content creators can also maximize their brand by giving users additional content—from digital postcards they can put on social media sites like Facebook to videos that users can watch and share anywhere. Some podcasts exist for shows that can be cross-promoted on various streaming platforms, enhancing the monetization of each brand.

This entire model, called transmedia, has been part of the video game ecosystem for a long time. And with the expansion of the Metaverse, it will become a game-changing opportunity for creators to engage their superusers or whales. This ecosystem can turn $20 in spending on Netflix per month into $200 per month and benefit the creative producers who benefit from higher royalty streams and cross-channel promotion.

Who wouldn't want to make more money? A company can triple its top-line revenue by getting 20 percent of consumers to spend ten times more on content (and they tend to engage in that level of spending).

For example, if a company has one hundred users spending $20 on a show, that will generate $2,000. But if 20 percent are willing to spend an additional $200, that will generate an additional $4,000. That's a 3x return from the existing platform's revenue model.

This is all a simple exercise in knowing the customer. However, the current platforms have been more concerned about the overall number of users than understanding the superusers. This could be for various reasons, including the traditional modeling exercises of Wall Street and venture capital analysts trying to assign value to a company's revenue streams. It's easier to valuate each user than to dig deeper into understanding the spending behaviors of the top 20 percent of customers.

> # IF A COMPANY HAS ONE HUNDRED USERS SPENDING $20 ON A SHOW, THAT WILL GENERATE $2,000. BUT IF 20 PERCENT ARE WILLING TO SPEND AN ADDITIONAL $200, THAT WILL GENERATE AN ADDITIONAL $4,000. THAT'S A 3X RETURN FROM THE EXISTING PLATFORM'S REVENUE MODEL.

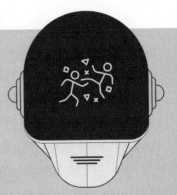

The Metaverse will likely push content creators into better understanding those users, particularly as users embrace complementary digital experiences and digital items. I anticipate that the music and film studios will remain when the Metaverse reaches its full potential. However, content creators can expand on their existing contracts with these third parties, engage their whale customers, and dramatically increase their revenue potential thanks to technology that largely exists already.

Today, 80 percent of revenue in video games comes from the top 20 percent of consumers. However, Netflix, Apple, and Microsoft don't embrace this principle. Currently, Netflix, Apple, and Microsoft aim to create various video game streaming services that set a fixed amount of money per month for all users.

Some superusers might be willing to pay $120 per month, but these streaming services might cost just $15 per month. Again, this might be good for the average consumer, but it would only commoditize the video gaming sector and push developers into a work-for-hire situation.

In addition, this is not a sustainable model for Microsoft and Apple for certain games. And based on the existing success of the video gaming industry, I doubt developers will want to put themselves into a situation like what musicians have faced for decades.

The 80/20 principle will be a major force in the Metaverse economy as the music, film, and publishing industries start to embrace their under-monetized buyers.

That's the future, and for artists in all fields, it's life-changing news.

SCAN ME FOR MORE INFO

CHAPTER 5

HOW VIDEO GAMES SAVED THE WORLD

Imagine an elite team of Navy SEALs standing in the woods. They're one hundred yards from a guarded compound in a remote mountain region. They're more than seven thousand miles from Annapolis, Maryland (home of the United States Naval Academy).

It's dark. The temperatures are freezing. Owls are hooting. The SEALs can see their breath.

Snow covers the ground. Ice layers the fir trees. One SEAL touches the snow, which drops from his hand like sand in an hourglass. Beside him, another SEAL uses night-vision technology to spy on enemy combatants patrolling the compound—where a fellow SEAL is being held hostage. The SEAL spies the silhouettes of two armed men standing by the main gate, one on the roof smoking a cigarette, and two sleeping on a bench by the front door. A dog runs out of the compound, chasing a rabbit toward a stump.

"How many are inside?" the lead officer asks.

One SEAL lowers his eyes to a screen controlling a drone that hovers over the compound. It looks down to see into the building and captures the heat maps of four individuals, including one sleeping in a corner—assumed to be the captured SEAL. "Four," he whispers. "Three enemies. Target is in sight. The second room on the left."

"On my signal," the officer says. He raises and then drops an arm. The SEALs swarm the compound, quietly subduing the militants outside. They breach the walls, communicating silently through hand signals. They locate a window, enter the compound, and make their way to where they believe their fellow SEAL waits.

They conduct their typical sweeping actions when entering a compound, covering all sides as they move from room to room. But before they enter the final room, an alarm sounds and a gun goes off. Unfortunately, the drone failed to register a fifth person in the building, a militant hiding in the kitchen with a rifle.

The room and everything in it—including the SEALs and the enemy combatant—freeze in place.

This has all been an intensive virtual and augmented reality *simulation*.

The simulation was conducted entirely through video game technology that allows military officials and SEALs to practice skills and tactics in a controlled environment.

The purpose: to prepare them for real-world scenarios like this one.

The SEALs were wearing headsets in an open training facility. No one was hurt. No one was injured. Maybe someone's ego was bruised. However, they learned a valuable lesson—don't rely solely on the drone hovering overhead; it may make a mistake. Practicing every scenario and learning every possible lesson is essential in a life-or-death situation.

These virtual simulations were not possible twenty, even ten, years ago, but they will be very soon. Today, the military uses similar simulations to recruit SEALs and train officers how to shoot

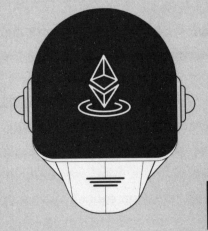

VIDEO
GAMES
HAVE
CHANGED THE WORLD.
IN FACT, I'LL GO
FURTHER AND
SAY THIS:
VIDEO GAMES
ARE NOW
SAVING THE WORLD.

weapons at augmented targets off a ship.[56] These tools prove the dramatic impact video games and their interlinked technologies have on this world.

While some people may dismiss the power of video games or associate them with young men playing war games, I stress that this is just one niche in a growing industry.

Video games have changed the world.

In fact, I'll go further and say this: video games are now *saving the world*.

ARE YOU NOT ENTERTAINED?

How have video games saved the world?

There have been obvious effects over the last thirty years. First, consider the growth of the entertainment world. As I noted in the previous chapter, the revenue model of video games dwarfs the size of the film, book, and music industries. This is a $200 billion industry that has shaped culture, created successful franchise models, and united communities around the globe.

Next, let's look at education, another important sector that video games have influenced positively. Video games have dramatically altered the future of education, providing students of all ages access to unique lessons that can be customized to their learning style. Games are essential tools in early education and can help young students learn the basics of math, reading, science, language skills, and much more. And they have evolved to educate everyone from preschool students to postgraduate and doctoral students working on some of the greatest challenges in the world.

Let's start with engineering. Video gaming engines facilitate education around architectural design and visualization, with 3D models and simulations of city planning. These video games and educational simulations are critical for cities that must better understand their use of land and resource management.

Developers are also creating advanced applications for medical professionals like surgeons. New educational programs—based on video game software and technology—might include spending hundreds of hours training on procedures in a simulated environment. In the future, your surgeon will have practiced your operation in a digital space hundreds of times—and you'll likely experience a better outcome as a result. These technologies will save lives, improve surgeries, and quickly replace current training opportunities and educational standards in medicine. These technologies will save lives and improve surgeries.

The education opportunities expand beyond the traditional workforce and exist in many other places of societal importance. Take environmental awareness, for example. Video games now educate players about environmental issues and promote conservation efforts. They can help to raise awareness about important environmental topics and inspire players to act. Video game applications also help officials engage in crisis or disaster scenarios like floods, earthquakes, and hurricanes. These vital training simulations help emergency response individuals know where to allocate resources, where to avoid dangers, and how to respond to victims quickly.

So when I say *video games are saving the world*, I'm not being hyperbolic. I'll explain in the next chapter on Metasites how the Metaverse will take us even further and help us to better understand the impact of human beings on our earth, increase environmental and social awareness, and drive more charitable opportunities to create real change.

And what about health?

Many video games now teach people how to improve their physical and mental health. For example, video games have been proven to help individuals cope with depression and anxiety.[57] Stroke victims have also used them to relearn how to manage the motion and movement of limbs. There are countless applications of video games in today's health environment. I haven't even started to describe the cognitive and social benefits of gaming in today's hyperconnected society.

Of course, all these positive benefits would only be possible with the technology that the video game sector can claim as its own over the last few decades.

YOUR DIGITAL WORLD, BROUGHT TO YOU BY VIDEO GAMES

The video game industry—valued at roughly $200 billion—has come a long way since the creation of the first game.[58] Back in 1958—physicist William Higinbotham used an oscilloscope to create a game called *Tennis for Two* to display the capabilities of his laboratory's new computer. Higinbotham, who worked at the Brookhaven National Laboratory, operated an IBM 704, a mainframe system about the size of a washing machine. His game featured a two-dimensional tennis court with a single horizontal line that acted as a net and two additional lines that acted as the edges of the court. Competitors would use knobs to hit a single dot back and forth across the net with two on-screen "tennis rackets." *Tennis for Two* was a precursor to *Spacewar!*, which was created in 1962 by Steve Russell and is widely considered the first real video game.

Most people know video games based on their age and generation. For example, anyone born in the 1970s may have memories of the Atari 2600, as the creation of home-console gaming was the second major step for the industry over the last sixty years.

Children from the 1980s will remember the greater accessibility and improved graphics of the original Nintendo Entertainment System and its iconic characters from *Super Mario*, *Donkey Kong*, *The Legend of Zelda*, and more.

By the 2000s, video gaming technology had grown by leaps and bounds. Home-console graphics improved dramatically under the advancement of the PlayStation and Xbox consoles. Video games have consistently been a part of every generation's life since the 1970s, and they are not something that people have grown out of. After all, there are more than three billion players in the world today—and that number is growing.

Meanwhile, improved digital internet speeds helped fuel the rise of online gaming. The digitalization of high-speed internet popularized online interaction through console games like *Halo*, which allowed remote teams of players to engage in a capture-the-flag-style shooting match. This was also a period when players could compete against each other online via sports franchises like *Madden NFL*, *FIFA*, and other popular platforms.

As mobile speeds improved, giving way to smartphones, mobile gaming surged at the onset of the century. The proliferation of smartphones and similar devices helped propel mobile gaming to the forefront of revenue generation for the industry. Now, we are entering the next major stage of development—one that incorporates virtual and augmented reality. These technologies can and will create more immersive experiences that transcend the imaginations of even the most advanced gamers of today's generation.

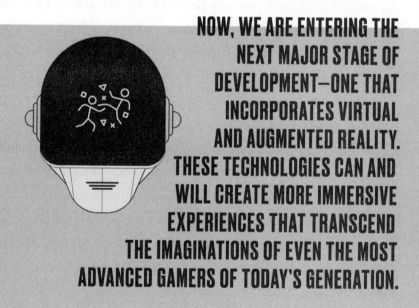

NOW, WE ARE ENTERING THE NEXT MAJOR STAGE OF DEVELOPMENT—ONE THAT INCORPORATES VIRTUAL AND AUGMENTED REALITY. THESE TECHNOLOGIES CAN AND WILL CREATE MORE IMMERSIVE EXPERIENCES THAT TRANSCEND THE IMAGINATIONS OF EVEN THE MOST ADVANCED GAMERS OF TODAY'S GENERATION.

However, I want to take a step back and discuss how these technologies have altered other industries. Let me draw a straight line between the video game sector and a company like electric vehicle manufacturer Tesla.

My observations and analysis might surprise a company like Tesla.

There is an incredible focus today on the future of self-driving cars and artificial intelligence. Both technologies will raise standards of living, improve productivity, and boost economic growth in societies around the world. They wouldn't be possible without the video gaming industry.

Why? Let's start with a semiconductor (computer chip) manufacturer called NVIDIA.

In 1993, NVIDIA's CEO, Jen-Hsun Huang, launched a company that would build specialized semiconductor chips to create faster and more realistic graphics for video games. At the time, his team recognized that no real market existed for these products. However, they had the foresight to understand that a wave of demand would come.

Initially, they focused on a burgeoning market for products called graphics processing units (GPUs). These are additional chips that video game users can plug into their desktop computer's motherboard to turbocharge their video game experience, creating ultra-fast graphics and improved game quality.

NVIDIA has long focused on graphics and computing semiconductors for the video gaming industry. The company started in the video game space to build its business and clout before pivoting toward other sectors. However, certain investors and would-be partners didn't share much enthusiasm for the video game space. Nevertheless, the company did find some initial success in other graphic-intensive applications like 3D modeling and video editing.

However, the application of these tools quickly evolved. As a result, two decades later, GPUs became essential to new industries that required immense computing power, improved graphics, and heightened user experience.

By 2012, NVIDIA chips powered the digital dashboard of the Tesla electric sedan.[59] In recent years, NVIDIA's business has increasingly centered on artificial intelligence and machine learning. The same high-performance GPUs for graphics in video games are equally crucial for training and running machine-learning models, which makes them ideal for deep-learning applications. In 2022, NVIDIA announced a partnership with Microsoft to build massive cloud artificial intelligence supercomputers in a multiyear collaboration project.[60]

How can that change the future of the world? Deep learning and artificial intelligence could one day allow computers to program by themselves and not need anyone to code by hand. This can fuel new technologies like advanced search, digital speech, image recognition, and, ultimately, deeply immersive experiences in the Metaverse.

> DEEP LEARNING AND ARTIFICIAL INTELLIGENCE COULD ONE DAY ALLOW COMPUTERS TO PROGRAM BY THEMSELVES AND NOT NEED ANYONE TO CODE BY HAND. THIS CAN FUEL NEW TECHNOLOGIES LIKE ADVANCED SEARCH, DIGITAL SPEECH, IMAGE RECOGNITION, AND, ULTIMATELY, DEEPLY IMMERSIVE EXPERIENCES IN THE METAVERSE.

NVIDIA is just a part of one of the most important variables of life: *speed*.

Today, the cell phone in your pocket contains more powerful technology than what launched the *Apollo 11* rocket. Similarly, schoolchildren are doing their homework on Apple computers that are infinitely faster than the early Mac iterations of the 1990s that launched the home-computer revolution. We must thank the video game technology players for this.

The superfast computers we have today are the result of video games. In fact, artificial intelligence—which has generated a significant amount of attention in recent years due to the arrival of ChatGPT—has accelerated due in part to a project called DeepMind. This program teaches artificial intelligence by having it play video games.

Considering the technologies of the last twenty-five years, most started with very simple interfaces and purposes. The Apple MacBook was designed for office applications and word processing. The iPhone was devised for text, music, and audio communication. But further iterations of these technologies centered on the integration of video gaming. The first iPad iteration was designed for digital books and magazines. The second version—with its more advanced computing power and graphical capacity—centered on playing games and integrating with the company's App Store. While Apple had little interest in developing many video games for its hardware, Apple's first demo centered on video games because the company wanted to sell third-party games in its store. In fact, during its iPad demo, the presentation featured a button to access its game arcade and another to access its App Store for game purchases.

We already know that gaming will remain at the center of virtual reality experiences in the future. VR headsets with fast speeds and advanced networking provide an immediate, immersive 360-degree audiovisual perspective. You feel, right away, that you're in the center of the game: playing the sport, fighting the battle, or exploring the world.

As Meta Platforms CEO Mark Zuckerberg pushes for more adoption of his company's headsets, video games have been critical for revenue and user interest. The Meta Quest Pro headsets have succeeded in shooting games like *The Walking Dead*, music games like *Beat Saber*, and city simulation games like *Lil Cuties*.

Over time, virtual reality and graphical improvements—largely fueled by video gaming technology and software advancements—will get us more technology to train individuals around manufacturing in augmented reality or to allow surgeons to engage remotely. That time is coming, and video game technology will lead the way.

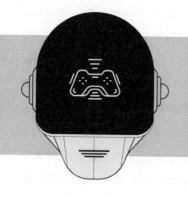

THAT TIME IS COMING, AND VIDEO GAME TECHNOLOGY WILL LEAD THE WAY.

This takes me to the professional importance of VR and simulation technology. For example, there might be no industry that stands to benefit more from this technology than aviation.

Today, the aviation industry faces a great challenge. Consultancy Oliver Wyman says that the global industry will be short eighty thousand pilots by 2032, primarily due to retirement, growing demand, and the challenge of finding willing employees.[61] One of the biggest hurdles to hiring new pilots is education and flying time.

But video games are meeting this challenge and saving this industry. Today, the game *X-Plane* offers a realistic simulation of flying different airplanes. In fact, multiple studies have shown that *Microsoft Flight Simulator*, a consumer-centric game first released in 1982, can enhance the education and training of private and commercial pilots.[62] The video game sector has enabled pilots to train in virtual environments, which are safer than traditional sessions and more cost-effective.

Advancements in technology provide deeply immersive graphics and physics engines that accurately replicate the movements and experience of physical aircraft. Pilots can receive training in various scenarios, including takeoff, landing, and emergency procedures. Video games have complemented existing simulation strategies in robust ways as well. For example, video games promote interactive training modules that teach new skills or refresh existing ones through nearly any available screen.

X-Plane won't just help train professional airline pilots. When engineers design spaceships or flying cars, they can use *X-Plane* as the simulator to test the devices' capabilities. Should flying cars finally reach the testing stages, we will already have a physically realistic simulation for the flights.

Finally, it's worth noting that the payment systems in video games are already driving integration in other industries. Currently, blockchain adoption is quickly happening in the video game industry. Blockchain wallets (which I'll explain in greater detail in the next chapter) make it possible for people to take digital currencies, wallets, and items with them through digital worlds. Mass adoption of the blockchain will likely happen through video games before they become mainstream in other places around the world.

BY THE WAY, VIDEO GAMES ARE GOOD FOR YOU

I want to discuss the final way video games have saved the world.

In the wake of COVID-19, video games have exploded in popularity. As I mentioned earlier, there are currently 3.2 billion video game players worldwide. Now, there will be people who disagree with me—mainly due to a stigma that still exists around gaming—but I believe video games have created environments for extremely healthy social interaction.

The last twenty years have allowed individuals to discover people with similar passions, interests, and views worldwide. If you're from a small town of one thousand people, you might not find a single person, let alone ten people, who likes your taste in music, art, or gaming. That said, the global community of 3.2 billion players—on top of extensive social networks—has formulated a real opportunity for connection among like-minded individuals.

Today, players can work and play together online.

Furthermore, there is plenty of scientific data to show that video games help players manage stress and improve their moods. Evidence shows that video games help improve cognitive function, reasoning, memory, and problem-solving skills. For example, a 2020 study from four doctors in Spain determined that patients overcoming chemotherapy experienced a 30 percent reduction in pain by playing video games.[63] Additionally, a 2022 study, supported by the National Institute on Drug Abuse (NIDA) and other entities of the National Institutes of Health (NIH), found that children playing video games for three hours per day showed better results on "cognitive skills tests involving impulse control and working memory compared to children who had never played video games."[64] Lastly, ample evidence exists suggesting that games provide incredible cognitive, physical, and emotional benefits to senior citizens.[65]

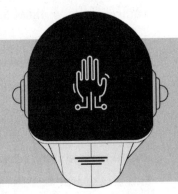

VIDEO GAMES HELP IMPROVE COGNITIVE FUNCTION, REASONING, MEMORY, AND PROBLEM-SOLVING SKILLS.

While I stress that everyone should enjoy their game playing in moderation and choose age-appropriate games, these results cannot be ignored. Furthermore, I want to stress the importance of video games in team building and how parents might consider managing their children's video gaming practices.

It might be expected for parents to tell their children to stop playing a game immediately, unplug, and walk away. In today's environment of online, collaborative games, like *Fortnite*, many involve teams and team management. Consider the scenario if your child was on a basketball team and had a game. You wouldn't take them home in the middle of the game, would you? It doesn't make sense to do that in video games either.

It's the same as pulling a child off the court. It places a child in a position where they are letting teammates down. So, instead, I recommend we tell children to finish a round and not start the next one, ensuring a proper ending to the game. Through gaming, these important lessons can be learned early in life: teamwork, commitment, and collaborative problem-solving. And in many small ways, each lesson can lead to a better and brighter future.

THE TECHNOLOGY OF TODAY'S VIDEO GAMES AND TOMORROW'S METAVERSE

So far, we've covered the critical elements of the Metaverse, its primary actors, and the technologies central to its success. Next, we will explore further integration of physical reality and virtual spaces and the technologies that will bring this convergence together.

Video games have already brought dramatic advancements in VR and AR technologies. This technology will be critical to establishing immersive virtual experiences. NVIDIA's graphics cards—and others like them—have produced high-quality 3D graphics and animation that will create realistic and visually appealing digital spaces.

Further, NVIDIA's advancements in AI and machine learning will help produce intelligent virtual characters capable of communication and will help develop complex virtual environments capable of unlimited customization. That AI will also enable natural language processing, allowing users to communicate with virtual characters. The existing networking and online technologies that currently power video gaming networks will soon support large numbers of users and their avatars assembling simultaneously in virtual space. And blockchain, which is already critical to the video gaming economy, will act as a mechanism to record interactions, enable payments in the Metaverse economy, and ensure trust and accountability among users.

Video games are already facilitating the most immersive and engaging technology available today. As such, these technologies should be adopted to maximize positive outcomes for the next iteration of the internet and the possibilities for users to immerse themselves in the Metaverse. And nowhere will that immersion experience be more important than in the Metasites that will rock your world.

SCAN ME FOR MORE INFO

CHAPTER 6

WHY METASITES WILL ROCK YOUR WORLD

In 1998, Nobel Prize-winning economist Paul Krugman offered a dire warning to investors about an emerging technology that had just begun to expand across the United States. He asserted that the *internet*, still in its infancy, would provide little value to the future of the global—let alone the US—economy. Krugman wrote,

> The growth of the Internet will slow drastically, as the flaw in "Metcalfe's law"—which states that the number of potential connections in a network is proportional to the square of the number of participants—becomes apparent: most people have nothing to say to each other! By 2005 or so, it will become clear that the Internet's impact on the economy has been no greater than the fax machine's.[66]

Of course, by 2005, the internet had become a revolutionary technology that had already changed the future of commerce, communication, and connectivity. It turns out that people had a lot to say to each other, and many businesses had evolved from the physical world to the digital landscape. E-commerce has since grown at a breakneck pace.

Krugman isn't alone in predicting that an emerging technology wouldn't provide incredible benefits for business and humanity. Naysayers fill the history books. Dr. Dionysius Lardner, a famous astronomy professor at University College London, said in 1830 that high-speed rail travel was impossible and would leave passengers struggling to breathe.[67] In 1859, business associates of Edwin Drake—the first American to successfully drill for oil—said anyone digging into the ground in search of oil was crazy (they even called Edwin "Crazy Drake").[68] Western Union wrote in 1876 that the telephone had "too many shortcomings to be seriously considered as a means of communication," while US president Rutherford B. Hayes later said, "It's a great invention, but who would want to use it anyway?"[69] Astronomer Simon Newcomb said in 1902 that airplane travel was "unpractical and insignificant, if not utterly impossible."[70]

Actor and director Charlie Chaplin called cinema "little more than a fad."[71] Ken Olsen of Digital Equipment Corporation said in 1977, "there is no reason for any individual to have a computer in the home."[72] And *Newsweek* magazine's Clifford Stoll said in 1995, "the truth is no online database will replace your daily newspaper."[73]

These experts were proven wrong as these technologies fueled progress.

The same year that Krugman authored the notorious column predicting the internet's lackluster impact, entrepreneurs Sergey Brin and Larry Page founded Google in Menlo Park, California. Five years prior, NVIDIA began its ascent into the global gaming industries and quickly turbocharged the connectivity of global networks. Amazon emerged in 1994 as an online portal for publishers to sell books directly to consumers, paving its way for global dominance in e-commerce three decades later. And Facebook—which reached a $1 trillion market cap in 2021—started in a small Harvard dorm room in 2004, a year before the internet's economic impact was predicted to rival the fax machine.[74]

Looking back, many digital entrepreneurs who shaped today's digital economy didn't know where the future would take them. Still, they remained optimistic that network technology would become faster, more powerful, and more inclusive. And they anticipated (and assumed) that more humans would adopt the internet as a tool as access expanded to new markets. Now, it's impossible to imagine global commerce without the internet.

In 1998, the internet had 147 million users, a figure that represented just 3.6 percent of the global population. By 2005, when Krugman's prediction failed to materialize, that figure had increased to 888 million—or 13.9 percent of the global population, according to Internet World Stats.[75] In April 2023, the number of worldwide internet users grew to 5.18 billion, or 64.6 percent of the global population. In addition, the number of mobile users hit 5.48 billion, representing over 68 percent of the world's population.[76]

It's easy to snicker at Krugman's prediction.

But one must think about life before the internet. In many nations, the world was previously closed off. When the internet arrived, it opened doors for people that they previously didn't think were possible. Thank goodness Krugman was wrong and that those entrepreneurs were right.

LOOKING BACK, MANY DIGITAL ENTREPRENEURS WHO SHAPED TODAY'S DIGITAL ECONOMY DIDN'T KNOW WHERE THE FUTURE WOULD TAKE THEM. STILL, THEY REMAINED OPTIMISTIC THAT NETWORK TECHNOLOGY WOULD BECOME FASTER, MORE POWERFUL, AND MORE INCLUSIVE. AND THEY ANTICIPATED (AND ASSUMED) THAT MORE HUMANS WOULD ADOPT THE INTERNET AS A TOOL AS ACCESS EXPANDED TO NEW MARKETS. NOW, IT'S IMPOSSIBLE TO IMAGINE GLOBAL COMMERCE WITHOUT THE INTERNET.

Of course, with every new technology or iteration, some people reject its viability and potential. In the beginning days of Twitter (recently rebranded as "X"), critics questioned why users would limit themselves to social media statements spanning just 140 characters. Yet by Q2 2022, Twitter had more than 200 million monetizable daily active users around the world.[77]

When YouTube was purchased by Google for $1.6 billion in 2006, the video platform's founders filmed a video—in which they appeared stunned by the acquisition's value—in the parking lot of the search giant's headquarters.[78] Initially, the deal didn't seem logical given the immense price tag. Just seventeen years later, YouTube's value stands between $180 billion and $300 billion, depending on the source and estimate.[79] Not only has the economic impact of the internet surpassed that of the fax machine, but it also has no equal.

So, when I and others say the Metaverse is potentially worth $10 trillion to $30 trillion, I stress that our figures could be on the low side in the long run. Any company doubting the Metaverse's potential and dismissing its viability may soon find itself on the outside looking in on a revenue-generating technology unlike anything in the history of our economy.

IT STARTS WITH THE METASITE

In a previous chapter, I briefly described Metasites as the mechanism that will provide unique utility and value to creatives when the Metaverse reaches its potential. Metasites are the backbone of the Metaverse's future and potential for your success.

Pay attention.

If you missed out on Instagram, ignored Twitter, failed to create a YouTube channel, or flaked on other groundbreaking technologies, Metasites will deliver an opportunity for redemption. Metasites will turbocharge the economy unlike anything we've witnessed in history. And they'll empower businesses and consumers like never before.

This is the real estate and technology suite that will propel your future.

METASITES WILL TURBOCHARGE THE ECONOMY UNLIKE ANYTHING WE'VE WITNESSED IN HISTORY. AND THEY'LL EMPOWER BUSINESSES AND CONSUMERS LIKE NEVER BEFORE.

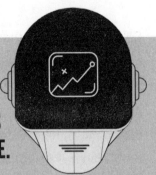

To understand Metasites, one must acknowledge three underlying technologies that power existing virtual worlds—like *Roblox*, *World of Warcraft*, and *Fortnite*—and will serve as the basis for future Metasites. The first technology is the real-time rendering power of a computer or game console. The second technology is cloud gaming. Today's cloud computing makes it possible for computational work on remote servers without the high costs of physical hardware. This rendering power helps us enter digital worlds without delay. Finally, we need to understand the third technology, behind the portal, which allows us to travel from one virtual world to the next. Think of it as being able to walk through one door or elevator and enter a new virtual world. Thanks to existing technology, we'll transition from a 2D to a 3D world.

Metasites are the direct descendants of the traditional websites we have known during the first and second iterations of the internet.

Today, you know websites by their domain names. For example, you might visit ESPN.com to read about sports, watch game highlights, or follow your favorite teams. You might visit your favorite musician's website to watch music videos, purchase concert tickets, or read about their latest projects. You might log onto

CNN.com to read the news, listen to opinions on politics and culture, or explore exotic locations in its travel section.

Each page on the website features a link that directs you to a different page. And each page is viewed through two-dimensional experiences, regardless of the screen on which you visit. You can visit these sites from any digital device supporting web browsers like Firefox, Safari, Chrome, or Edge. But once you experience the immersive nature of a Metasite, these browsers will feel like relics in less than ten years. In twenty years, you'll tell younger generations about what life was like before the Metaverse or the first time you visited a Metasite. You'll talk about how you had to sign onto a computer, type in a website destination, use a physical mouse or trackpad, and even—*GASP!*—click away pop-up ads that interrupted your internet "surfing" (another dying term).

Yes, you'll sound like previous generations who went to libraries, checked out books using the Dewey decimal system, and wrote college papers on typewriters.

Don't worry; I'll be doing the same thing with my grandchildren, telling them how long it took for a 4G phone to download a song—a whole thirty-five seconds!

That's because the next iteration of websites—Metasites—will completely blow your mind and alter your experience as a visitor to these digital destinations. Rather than just visiting a website, you'll be immersed in a platform of three-dimensional gaming, shopping, events, and socialization. You'll be "visiting" virtual destinations that take you directly to the source of your interests. For example, rather than watching sports highlights on a website video platform, you'll watch the action from a virtual location that takes you inside the game itself. Think about sitting center court at a National Basketball Association game or at the fifty-yard line at the Super Bowl.

Users will have the capacity to experience the Metaverse across any screen, with video game technology powering the virtual and augmented reality experiences. The Metaverse will work on mobile—which is important for interoperability and users' capacity to take digital items with them wherever they go. However, I argue that consumers will prefer to experience the great details of the Metaverse on the bigger screens of glasses or TV.

And the optimal experience will likely be within digital caves.

Now, let me offer you my vision of what this technology will look like.

These digital caves will be the size of a traditional walk-in closet, featuring a large variety of sensors, cameras, and projection screens. Some of these caves will be portable, built like a pop-up tent of aluminum columns and felt screens. Others will be more expensive, built into portions of a home or apartment. These caves—through rendering technology and cloud-based computing—will allow users to instantly immerse themselves into a digital environment that rivals real-world locations or digital experiences created by content producers. For example, you'll be able to stand in the Sistine Chapel as the digital cave converts into that living museum in the Vatican. Then, instead of typing in a new website extension, you can tell your cave and computer to take you thousands of miles away to the Himalayas. The caves will go beyond physical tourist experiences. They will act as the vessel for experiences in gaming, education, and even live events such as concerts, much like the holodeck on *Star Trek*.

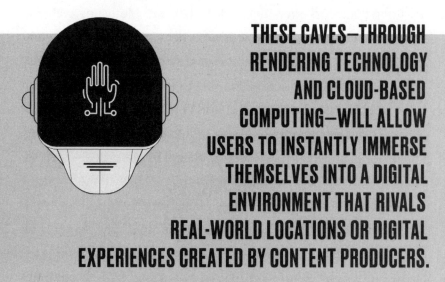

THESE CAVES—THROUGH RENDERING TECHNOLOGY AND CLOUD-BASED COMPUTING—WILL ALLOW USERS TO INSTANTLY IMMERSE THEMSELVES INTO A DIGITAL ENVIRONMENT THAT RIVALS REAL-WORLD LOCATIONS OR DIGITAL EXPERIENCES CREATED BY CONTENT PRODUCERS.

The other important component of Metasites is what I discussed earlier in chapter 3—the interoperability of the networks. As I noted, Metasites will allow you to bring digital items from one world to another world, aligning the economies across Metasites. This interoperability is critical to the functionality and confidence of the Metaverse. As I'll explain in the coming chapters on blockchain and digital wallets, users must be able to take souvenirs, digital memorabilia, and more across the various networks to create a fully immersive experience that optimizes revenue and realism for brands, users, and consumers.

These Metasites will allow you to explore virtual environments and engage in content and products like never before. They will be built on cloud rendering, interoperability, and the extension of AR and VR tech into the real world.

I don't want to offer the simple idea that Metasites will just resemble the real world or the environment around you. It's more than just watching sports or attending concerts in digital stadiums. These sites can take virtually any form—from real to imaginative, from futuristic cities to gaming worlds in *Fortnite* or other platforms. They may resemble the sets of television shows, the edges of the world, or even the moon. The design of Metasites—and the specific experiences that exist—will all come down to the creators and the content they wish to share with an audience.

Digital consultancy Gartner projects that 25 percent of consumers will use the Metaverse every day by 2026, setting the stage for aggressive growth among brands seeking to cultivate new customers.[80] Given that we're so close to this new future, we need to explore and showcase the possibilities of Metasites through a few simple examples. To get your imagination going around the Metaverse's possibilities, I'm going to share three case studies. First, we'll explore two well-known brands—Adidas and Crate & Barrel—that have a major head start in the Metaverse. I'll explain how Metasites will create not only unforgettable experiences for users but also opportunities for these brands to increase revenue potential—while expanding on their existing physical operations. Finally, for good measure, I'll discuss how musicians can succeed through a case study of a band about to take the Metaverse by storm.

CASE STUDY 1: GO FOR THE GOAL WITH ADIDAS

The Metaverse has shifted the intense rivalry of consumer brands from the physical world to the virtual one. Over time, it will take us from the fierce retail battles at the shoe store to the digital battle on Metasites. I struggle to think of two brands that will engage in a bigger battle than Nike and Adidas.

Nike has already established itself as a leader in the early days of the Metaverse. It is selling digital items for avatars, NFTs, and collectors' items; it has established a presence in various digital worlds like *Fortnite*; and it has made the Metaverse a cornerstone of its digital strategy for the decade ahead.

So, how does a rival like Adidas respond? The answer will come when it builds a Metasite that creates a digital world that embodies the spirit and potential of the brand.

I would break this down into three major components of the brand itself: first, selling products for the physical world; second, selling products for the digital world; and third, creating brand experiences that drive customer retention and future sales. There are many reasons why individuals may want to partake in these experiences. They may want convenience, a major driver of e-commerce demand over the last fifteen years. They may crave the digital experience and the other possible perks of using this technology. Or their buying behaviors might have changed in the wake of the global COVID-19 pandemic, and they may prefer personal experiences that don't involve public spaces.

So, let's think about our first case study for Metasites.

Imagine that you want new shoes. That should be easy since the average American buys 7.4 pairs of shoes yearly, according to the American Apparel & Footwear Association.[81] Typically, you'd drive to the store, try on the product, and—assuming the shoes are in stock—purchase a pair that day. Or, if you know your shoe size, you might go on Amazon, order a pair, and have them arrive within two to five days. Let's hope they fit and that you like the look and feel. Otherwise, you'll be heading to the nearest UPS Store to return the product.

In the Metaverse, you might enter a digital cave or use a cell phone to access a Metasite built around the company's brand. You can enter a virtual store or click a few buttons on your phone, then point the camera at your feet and see how a specific pair looks on you. You can order the shoes then and there, have them delivered, and be on your way to your next soccer match with neighborhood friends.

In the past, companies like Nike and Adidas have created artificial scarcity of various sneaker lines, including Air Jordans and Yeezys, respectively. Only a certain number of these shoes exist. In the Metaverse, not only will users be able to purchase and own both physical and digital shoes, but they will also transact on blockchain technology that authenticates their ownership of these shoes and that a specific pair are real—not digital knock-offs—thanks to the scarcity of NFTs.

The same goes for your avatar traveling across Metasites, visiting with friends in digital experiences, and exhibiting your fashion sense. For example, the Adidas Metasite could allow you to try on various outfits, customize your avatar, and pay. In the case of projects by Nike, you could design virtual shoes with the company's branding and sell them through the company's digital stores.

These two examples empower customers to purchase products and exhibit a brand's meaning. The remaining portion of the customer experience is found in other areas of the Metaverse that I collectively call the *theme park*. I'm specifically talking about a place where brands can create experiences and charge customers for those experiences. On these sites, brands engage in entertainment. They might have a nightclub feel, live music offerings, or immersive experiences that give users the thrill of a lifetime.

For example, Adidas is one of the largest brands in the world for soccer or, as it's known outside the United States, football. Imagine immersive experiences that allow users to watch matches from the sidelines of stadiums around the globe—all while wearing customized Adidas shoes. You could even try your hand at goalie and take part in virtual shoot-outs against the world's top players. Consider branding events that take users to meet-and-greet events with leading athletes. Imagine cutting through the velvet rope and having access to live sporting events brought to you by these elite sports brands.

IMAGINE IMMERSIVE EXPERIENCES THAT ALLOW USERS TO WATCH MATCHES FROM THE SIDELINES OF STADIUMS AROUND THE GLOBE.

These Metasites will immerse sports fans into the environment and celebrate their favorite games, from Stamford Bridge (home of the Chelsea Blues) for Premier League matches in England to the

World Cup stadiums in 2026 and 2030. In addition, these Metasites will enhance the branding potential of top consumer brands and bring consumers closer to the action than ever.

CASE STUDY 2: CRATE & BARREL

The Metaverse extends beyond the theme park experiences I've described. As e-commerce continues to grow, these Metasites will expand and provide consumers with critical tools to make better-informed purchasing decisions. For this case study, we'll consider the Metaverse strategy of retailer Crate & Barrel. In May 2022, the company announced it was promoting its vice president of product design and development, Sebastian Brauer, to senior vice president for product design, development and *Metaverse*. With the new title, Brauer's responsibilities expanded to include "the company's strategic vision of the future Metaverse and web3."[82] Brauer has been a major advocate of blockchain technology and the digital transitions of brands. For a company like Crate & Barrel, the prospect of a digital showcase environment is a game changer. Rather than own expensive real estate or operate mall locations that have experienced a decline in physical traffic, a company like Crate & Barrel can build digital showrooms.

With Metasites, users may have their own site that resembles their physical home space. Crate & Barrel can provide a scalable room based on various dimensions that replicate the physical rooms of a user's home or apartment.

In a digital showcase room, users can browse products and see what furniture, artwork, and other Crate & Barrel products might look like in their homes. They can see if a piece of furniture will fit in a specific space or is the right style for the rest of the room. It also gives users the option to purchase products immediately.

Metasites for companies like Crate & Barrel could create incredible brand value and allow businesses to more effectively tell their stories. They have the potential to be significantly more powerful than today's traditional social media platforms. These Metasites put consumers directly in the room with the product. Instead of having a social media manager, every company will need to have a Metaverse brand manager in the next ten years.

CASE STUDY 3: SHURICK'S BAND, THE META VERSES

I have wanted to be a musician since I first heard Western songs on that $7 portable radio. But I was stuck playing the accordion. In the Metaverse, however, I have unlimited potential to get my virtual band off the ground. So, let me introduce you to my lyric-inspired band—The Meta Verses.

Whether musicians are just getting started or have a thirty-city tour planned for next year, a Metasite will provide them with unique opportunities to engage in audience development, digital sales, immersive events, and much more.

Musicians can create and customize a Metasite to create the allure and image of the band or individual. Guns N' Roses might have an edgier vibe, with their Metasite's primary location feeling like a whiskey bar. Meanwhile, a band like Imagine Dragons might set their site up to resemble an open music hall overlooking their hometown of Las Vegas, Nevada. These virtual spaces will create the initial feeling of the band's home location, a well-crafted image that hits the user upon entry and gives them a taste of what to expect from an aesthetic perspective. Within these Metasites, fans can instantly communicate with other fans via events that allow all users to explore the history and catalog of the band. These sites will enable bands to sell digital and physical merchandise like shirts, hats, and posters. Users might adorn their avatars in Rolling Stones shirts or purchase real shirts for delivery to their houses. It all comes down to the products and merchandise that bands offer in their digital stores—and the incredible opportunity for NFTs, which create unique value, exclusivity, and brand promotion for all participants in the Metaverse.

Digital content will sit at the heart of the Metasite experience for musicians. This can include selling music, pre-releasing songs, and allowing content producers to maximize revenue from their superusers (as explained in chapter 4). In addition, bands can host virtual concerts or meet-and-greets and provide other unique digital experiences that were previously unimaginable.

THE BENEFITS ARE LIMITLESS

Of course, these experiences aren't limited to musicians or other creative content generators. Any business—regardless of its size and reach—can benefit from the advancements of these Metasites. Small companies can create virtual stores to sell digital and physical goods. They can create interactive, virtual experiences that promote product launches, networking, and informational events. They can create communities around the subscribers and customers. The revenue-generating ideas around Metasites are still in their infancy, but I'd wager to say they are unlimited.

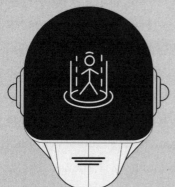

DITIGAL CONTENT WILL SIT AT THE HEART OF THE METASITE EXPERIENCE FOR MUSICIANS.

That said, it's not just about money. As I noted, the Metaverse will provide significant opportunity to showcase the efforts and successes of charitable organizations. One of the best use cases I can think of today is the ability to showcase the impact of climate change on the planet. Consider a future where you'll be able to experience demonstrations of what the earth will look like in one hundred years, two hundred years, or even five hundred years due to climate change. Imagine having an opportunity to see the impact of various scenarios on the planet. Metasites will allow users to travel into the future and see how the earth could look if we make a positive impact—and how it could look if we fail to act. In addition, consider the impact that charities can have by taking donors to locations in need and showing their efforts in action. Imagine walking through a village in Africa, seeing the positive effect of micro-donations on small businesses in emerging nations, and having impactful conversations with all parties.

This experience will not only allow donors to see their impact firsthand, but it can also heighten transparency, improve accountability, and allow others to measure the direct impact of their efforts in real time.

THE METASITE REAL ESTATE RUSH STARTS NOW

At the onset of the dot-com explosion, digital real estate became a massive market. As a result, speculators and companies rushed to secure domain names ending in .com, .org, and .net. These domains, along with others that have appeared as the internet has grown, identify a website's specific location on the World Wide

Web and serve as memorable destinations for users to explore content on today's internet.

As the Metaverse grows, the rush for digital real estate in Metasites will become another hotbed of speculation and development. Metasites will be the next extension of today's internet, acting as unique destinations within the virtual, immersive world of the future. These Metasites will maintain a unique number of portals allowing users to jump from one destination to another within the universe.

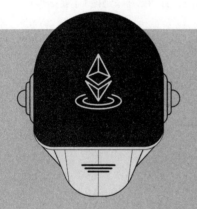

METASITES WILL BE THE NEXT EXTENSION OF TODAY'S INTERNET, ACTING AS UNIQUE DESTINATIONS WITHIN THE VIRTUAL, IMMERSIVE WORLD OF THE FUTURE.

Real estate in Manhattan, Hollywood, Chicago, and other commercial mall properties will continue to increase in value. Overhead costs, including energy, employees, and other fixed expenses, are likely to rise, not fall, in the years ahead. So, the opportunity for companies to transition their brand experiences from physical to digital Metasites can streamline costs and bring consumers closer to the brand. I expect template Metasites will cost roughly $250,000, while the investment for a brand-immersive site will average about $1 million at the onset. Over time, these costs will decline.

So, how will users purchase and develop their Metasites? One can expect Metasite development to operate similarly to previous websites. Users can build Metasites from scratch with tools and development resources offered by companies specializing in their generation. There could eventually be auctions or online real estate portals like the current physical real estate economy. In addition, some producers of Metasites might lease or rent their digital properties—again, like traditional, physical real estate in today's economy. Over time, this virtual economy will develop, creating unique opportunities for individuals to profit from the digital real estate that comprises the Metaverse.

Such transactions will be critical to the digital real estate of the future. And these transactions will operate on one necessary technology that establishes greater trust, authenticity, and speed in the Metaverse: the blockchain.

SCAN ME FOR MORE INFO

CHAPTER 7

UNDERSTANDING BLOCKCHAIN, BITCOIN, AND ETHEREUM

The Metaverse will create incredible consumer experiences, allowing users to move seamlessly between the real world and digital worlds. Users will be able to purchase digital goods and travel between these worlds with their favorite items, knowing that the underlying networks recognize their unique ownership.

As discussed in previous chapters, all this activity is projected to create an industry valued between $10 trillion to $30 trillion in revenue over the next decade. But that financial windfall won't operate on the traditional financial system you've known your entire life: banks, credit and debit cards, *or* cash.

Our focus so far has centered on the digital technologies that enabled the speed, power, and data management essential to the future Metaverse ecosystems. We've discussed the cloud-computing and graphics cards that powered the digital worlds of video games. We explored how visionary companies like NVIDIA established the framework for the video gaming ecosystems that would become the worlds of *Fortnite*, *Apex Legends*, *Minecraft*, and more.

But there's one critical technology we haven't discussed in depth yet that could be more important than all the graphics cards, cloud servers, and digital networks combined. It is the technology that will act as the financial backbone of the Metaverse.

It is called *blockchain*.

This tool will not only enable transactions and multitrillion dollars in commerce but will also protect your digital assets and allow you to take your unique items across various worlds (blockchain will be essential to interoperability and more).

Blockchain—as a concept—has existed since the early 1990s. However, the broad implementation of blockchain has emerged in the last decade with the widespread adoption of cryptocurrencies and platforms like Bitcoin and Ethereum.

If you don't know much about blockchain, Bitcoin, Ethereum, and other cryptocurrencies and platforms, the pages ahead will act as your "Blockchain 101" primer. Once you understand the power of blockchain, you will quickly understand how these technologies will create unrivaled economic opportunities for creative minds in the years ahead; protect users' identities, money, and possessions; and accelerate the development of this new world.

THE POWER BEHIND THE METAVERSE

It's essential to remember that the Metaverse itself will establish a new economy. The Metaverse will feature a digital economy unlike anything we've ever seen before in the history of humanity. But no economy is sustainable if it lacks a trustworthy financial network that encourages investment, future growth, and greater user adoption.

ONCE YOU UNDERSTAND THE POWER OF BLOCKCHAIN, YOU WILL QUICKLY UNDERSTAND HOW THESE TECHNOLOGIES WILL CREATE UNRIVALED ECONOMIC OPPORTUNITIES FOR CREATIVE MINDS IN THE YEARS AHEAD; PROTECT USERS' IDENTITIES, MONEY, AND POSSESSIONS; AND ACCELERATE THE DEVELOPMENT OF THIS NEW WORLD.

No economy can succeed if concerns about theft, corruption, or the insecurity of one's financial and personal assets persist. There is a reason why money flows into nations that have strong financial laws, accountability, and economic freedom. Individuals and companies move money offshore for multiple reasons, including concerns about autocrats and dictators, endless bureaucracy, extremely high taxation, corruption, or financial instability.

Blockchain technology will act as the secure financial infrastructure of the Metaverse. In fact, the Metaverse can't thrive without it. It will be essential for our digital lives—as we do everything in the Metaverse that we can do in real life. We'll engage in tourism. We'll meet new friends and hang out in new online business locations. We'll buy works of art like music, paintings, and films. We'll buy digital real estate. We'll buy consumer products in digital showrooms of companies like Crate & Barrel and have those products delivered to our physical address. But we need to ensure that every transaction is secure, transparent, and recognized by everyone participating in this economy. However, there isn't going to be a government or widespread regulators who are overseeing this new economy. Technology will need to solve most problems.

That's where blockchain enters the equation.

The concept is simple. Blockchain is effectively a long *chain* of information-gathering *blocks*, or a digital ledger that keeps records of transactions in sequential order. Once a transaction is stored on the blockchain, it will stay on the ledger for a period that enables confirmation. At any moment, buyers and sellers can look back at the blockchain's ledger and see the value and details behind that transaction. They will know exactly what is sold and for what price.

This transaction cannot be disputed. It cannot be unpublished. It is "official" forever.

When a block of information is completed and data is stored, the system generates a new block in the chain. The nature of that new block generation means that whatever transactions happen after the previous block will be sequential. There is no ability to alter the historical order of those transactions, which is very important in business and contract law.

Now, before we discuss the history of this technology and its primary use cases, I do want to address an important question:

would a company have any objection to using ledgers to store transactions and public information?

At first glance, there are challenges that must be overcome in the future. Today, companies and individuals might be wary of any public ledger that is available to any person using a network. Companies might not wish to release proprietary data on a blockchain, especially if it could technically be accessed by a third-party acting on behalf of someone using that network. For example, a company might worry that a competitor may gain insight into its business practices or customer interface. In addition, companies must properly establish rules around data privacy. That said, I anticipate these concerns will be addressed by the necessary parties as technology and the Metaverse mature, similarly to how concerns have been addressed in previous industries.

These principles are essential to understand, and they might require those learning about blockchain to explore more resources to grasp the basics.

Every participant in the Metaverse will have exposure to blockchain technology. It will be vital to the future of commerce. I believe it's essential that blockchain be taught in every high school in the United States, in every college financial and economics course, and—eventually—to younger students who must learn the importance of financial literacy.

Blockchain technology has the potential to upend the entire global banking system, making it possible to move money across borders without high remittance costs. Instead of paying a company like Western Union high fees to send money from one nation to another, blockchain can quickly transact, confirm, and

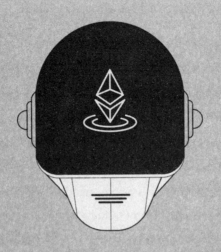

EVERY PARTICIPANT IN THE METAVERSE WILL HAVE EXPOSURE TO THE BLOCKCHAIN TECHNOLOGY. IT WILL BE VITAL TO THE FUTURE OF COMMERCE.

deliver money from one person to another thousands of miles away—almost instantly. As I'll explain, it could eliminate the need for most mid- and back-office roles at banks—especially those that involve the secure confirmation of traditional business transactions and exchange of property.

What does this mean?

Well, if we go back to the original foundation of blockchain technology, we can better observe the theory and implementation of blockchain and how it evolved into a financial-centric technology. Then, we can understand why it will be so essential to the Metaverse's development by a global network of independent users and businesses.

Phase One of blockchain started in 1991. At the time, two research scientists, Stuart Haber and W. Scott Stornetta, introduced the concept of blockchain with different terminology. Their goal was to create a technology that allowed for the timestamping of digital documents in a secure, decentralized location.

Think bank records, mortgage transaction logs, and even credit card payments. In simple terms, this timestamping could cut out the middlemen who confirmed and logged these financial activities at banks, mortgage companies, credit card organizations, and anywhere that bookkeeping was essential.

The timestamping and permanence of this storage would make it impossible for anyone to tamper or alter the data on the individual block in the ledger. In addition, the concept required no central authority, like a bank or government, to confirm the transaction—removing the need for more human activity in the process (or, in the case of government, cutting red tape and bureaucracy).

This technology's independence from a centralized authority became a critical feature of future iterations, and vital for the thousands of cryptocurrencies in existence in 2023.

That said, storing a single document on just one block at a time was inefficient. So, the following year, computer scientist Ralph Merkle created a company built on Stornetta and Haber's work. Merkle's cryptography would enable multiple documents and records to be stored in sequential order across a single block.

Over the next two decades, the concept of a ledger to record transactions advanced. But the biggest development occurred in 2008, when an anonymous author using the nom de plume Satoshi Nakamoto penned a white paper centered on the world's first decentralized peer-to-peer payment system and the model for what blockchain is today.

Phase Two of blockchain—centered on transactions—set the groundwork for the payment systems of the future. In 2009, that same anonymous author created Bitcoin and the first blockchain as a ledger.

To date, this mystery person has not been uncovered, although a handful of prominent technology experts and venture capitalists have claimed to be the author. Nakamoto's proposal to use a ledger to track transactions of a new digital currency was revolutionary. This ledger—giving access to anyone—established Bitcoin as the first decentralized digital cryptocurrency. It has recorded and confirmed every Bitcoin transaction ever made—all with total transparency, accountability, trust, and security.

For example, if someone purchases Bitcoin, that transaction is recorded on blockchain and global exchanges. In addition, this network operates on a system of nodes, or computers that use Bitcoin's software and confirm the transactions. Meanwhile, individuals who mine Bitcoin use computers operating computational math problems to receive the cryptocurrency as a reward.

These computers effectively compete to complete these mathematical problems, with the first to solve the problems receiving newly minted Bitcoins and transaction fees for their work. All new transactions are then stored on the blockchain and can never be altered or tampered with by participants. Meanwhile, these Bitcoins—which have financial value—create incentives for new miners to join the network and confirm transactions.

In 2020, Bitcoin experienced a dramatic bout of speculation. The price of one Bitcoin surged to more than $68,000 in 2021. By the end of 2022, as market turmoil increased and fears of a global recession emerged, the value of Bitcoin slumped back under $20,000. It's worth noting, however, that Bitcoin has experienced significant price volatility in the past. At the onset of Bitcoin's creation, when there were only a handful of users working on this experimental payment network, one of the first trades executed was 5,050 Bitcoins for $5.02 via PayPal. That means that the price of Bitcoin was once under a penny.[83]

A lot of people wonder what the price of Bitcoin should be. They focus on the utility value, but the reality is that the price of Bitcoin—and Ethereum—represents the speed of the network effect. It reflects the number of buyers and sellers coming in and out of the system.

This network effect is increasingly important for Ethereum and other networks on which the Metaverse will be built. As new users come online and require a specific cryptocurrency to develop new projects or spend money in the Metaverse, these values can and will appreciate. In addition, note that other cryptocurrencies can be directly converted to the US dollar and other currencies in the global markets.

A LOT OF PEOPLE WONDER WHAT THE PRICE OF BITCOIN SHOULD BE. THEY FOCUS ON THE UTILITY VALUE, BUT THE REALITY IS THAT THE PRICE OF BITCOIN— AND ETHEREUM—REPRESENTS THE SPEED OF THE NETWORK EFFECT. IT REFLECTS THE NUMBER OF BUYERS AND SELLERS COMING IN AND OUT OF THE SYSTEM.

But there is another critical element of Bitcoin that few people discuss. Bitcoin is a *decentralized* currency. No Wall Street bank like J.P. Morgan or central bank like the Federal Reserve controls it. In fact, both Bitcoin and Ethereum are deflationary monetary systems. This is an important point. Their existence is contrarian to modern economics, which helps ensure long-term appreciation in their value. Historically, the US dollar—a fiat currency—has lost more than 90 percent of its value over the last seventy years. Inflation of a fiat currency is effectively the result of government mismanagement that citizens have to pay for. This inflation is not possible with deflationary and decentralized cryptocurrencies.

Over time, Bitcoin will stop generating new Bitcoins for miners, meaning there will be a finite number of these specific coins. That limit, which the system will hit in 2140, will be twenty-one million Bitcoins. This is how Bitcoin was established, and because of its decentralized nature, it can never be changed.

Keep in mind, though, that buyers do not need to purchase an entire Bitcoin. Each Bitcoin is broken down into micro units called satoshis, named for the pseudonym of Bitcoin's mysterious founder. One hundred million satoshis equals one Bitcoin. So, buyers can purchase tiny amounts of Bitcoin anytime, and these transactions will be locked in Bitcoin's blockchain forever. That said, the finite nature of Bitcoin creates exclusivity, and the increasing adoption of Bitcoin has rivaled the adoption rate of the internet in the late 1990s. As Bitcoin grows more popular, it will expand its network effect, which further reduces the ability of a government to destroy it.

I'd argue that governments will never be able to eliminate Bitcoin from the global financial system. In addition, Bitcoin's first-move advantage in the global cryptocurrency markets has established a significant network effect. As of August 2022, there were more than 84 million blockchain wallets in existence, and all of them can buy and hold Bitcoin.[84]

Blockchain has many other potential use cases in the future outside of simple financial transactions. For example, it can register land ownership worldwide, eliminating quarrels and strengthening claims. Some nations have proposed its use for elections, creating transparent, secure entries that cannot be hacked.

It has also been proposed as a tool to register and track products across entire supply chains. For example, if you want to know the origin of your food—from farm to processing plant to your table—blockchain may provide that level of transparency.

Even more important, it will offer greater security and end the need for centralized payment and e-commerce networks. This security is linked to the ongoing need for better cybersecurity and trust in today's financial and digital commerce markets.

As I discussed in chapter 1, the Metaverse is the third iteration of the internet. The first iteration—Web 1.0—connected computers to large, centralized servers. It required gatekeepers like America Online to provide a platform for users to connect to servers to search and shop.

The second iteration—Web 2.0—was built on the back of centralized e-commerce platforms like Amazon, Apple's App Store, and Facebook. However, it also evolved through the large amounts of advertising that emerged from social media networks. These social media networks—which were free to users—harvested ample quantities of consumer data that companies could monetize by directing advertisements to their audiences. Keep in mind, if the product is free in Web 2.0, your data is typically the mechanism that pays for the product infrastructure.

In addition to Web 2.0 establishing massive, centralized e-commerce and social media platforms, it also fueled an environment that was dangerous for user data. The centralized nature of data collection made these troves of customer information valuable targets for hackers. As a result, over the last two decades, we've witnessed extremely large data breaches of centralized platforms like Facebook, Citigroup, Equifax, and more.

The Metaverse cannot succeed without the elimination of these massive breaches. Therefore, the reliance on decentralized programs, crypto assets, and blockchains that store and process transactions without the threat of hackers will become more and more important.

In late 2014, a critical development occurred that increased the viability of blockchain in multiple industries. It was called Blockchain 2.0, and it allowed for application development outside the cryptocurrency space. Blockchain was separated from technology. The following year, another cryptocurrency giant, Ethereum, emerged and introduced computer programs that operated within the individual blocks on the chain.

Ethereum is the second-largest cryptocurrency in the world. It is a blockchain like Bitcoin, with a few key advancements. Ethereum can be programmed on processes called *smart contracts*. These contracts are software programs that operate automatically when a specific condition occurs.

For example, you can establish ownership of artwork or an NFT, and no one else can claim ownership of that specific item. These so-called crypto assets include financial securities, digital currencies, NFTs, and other digital assets that can be exchanged for money. If someone agrees to purchase an asset, the transaction will be recorded on the Ethereum blockchain in the cryptocurrency known as Ether. These deals are then recorded for everyone to see and confirm. It's absolutely vital that individuals can verify their transactions to prove they purchased artwork, music, or other products.

Phase Three of blockchain emerged in 2017 when a group called EOS created a platform that established a new blockchain protocol. This protocol made it possible to develop decentralized applications—which will be critical to the development of the Metaverse. With decentralized applications, all new content developed can be simultaneously used by multiple participants.

This includes the dissemination and generation of new content, and ownership isn't limited to specific parties. This enables faster development of new programs. It also drives collaboration to create new standards and enables the feeding and seeding of content.

But these are just common examples often talked about at trade shows and on blogs trying to explain the basic concepts to most users. The reality is that blockchain is a database that cannot be destroyed and will achieve a network effect. So, think for a moment about all the things you can store on a database. We can store all sorts of knowledge that we never want to lose. Virtually anything can be stored on the blockchain so long as there is an incentive to do so. The challenge is that so many industries must adapt to the coming shifts in how customers operate.

For example, there was a time when consumers purchased movies in a physical format, like VHS and DVD. However, once Web 2.0 emerged and centralized players like Apple TV and Amazon Prime became dominant, users started to buy digital versions of movies that could be viewed only on these platforms.

Today, if you own a movie on Amazon Prime, you cannot transfer it to Apple. In the future, however, these purchases will be stored in a decentralized network—in a ledger—meaning that these companies will no longer have the power to keep a customer directly loyal (or even hostage) to their platform. Blockchain, as a technology that removes the centralized nature of the Web 2.0 business model, could therefore destroy powerful institutions.

I believe there will be a new public good when everything you buy on Apple can be translated to the blockchain. And if Amazon wants to have you as a customer, you can migrate that asset to Amazon. This could be incredibly disruptive to the business models found in the technology sector over the last fifteen years, and that's good for consumers.

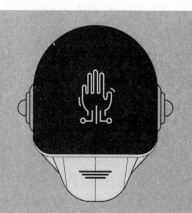

I BELIEVE THERE WILL BE A NEW PUBLIC GOOD WHEN EVERYTHING YOU BUY ON APPLE CAN BE TRANSLATED TO THE BLOCKCHAIN. AND IF AMAZON WANTS TO HAVE YOU AS A CUSTOMER, YOU CAN MIGRATE THAT ASSET TO AMAZON. THIS COULD BE INCREDIBLY DISRUPTIVE TO THE BUSINESS MODELS FOUND IN THE TECHNOLOGY SECTOR OVER THE LAST FIFTEEN YEARS, AND THAT'S GOOD FOR CONSUMERS.

WAIT, I HEARD THAT BITCOIN AND ETHEREUM WERE DANGEROUS

If you're new to Bitcoin or blockchain, you've probably heard about market problems in recent years. For example, in 2014, a massive $460 million hacking event transpired at a cryptocurrency exchange called Mt. Gox that—at the time—handled more than 70 percent of all Bitcoin transaction volume.[85] Since then, there have been several other hacking events that have occurred. In addition, you might have heard about the collapse of cryptocurrency exchanges in recent years.

Today's cryptocurrency exchanges are effectively banks that hold users' digital keys and cryptocurrency assets for them. They serve as a middleman or service to manage assets, and they've outright mismanaged those assets. It's important to note that these exchanges have no relationship with the underlying blockchain technology of various cryptocurrencies. In fact, a popular cryptocurrency exchange called FTX nearly collapsed the entire cryptocurrency market after rampant fraud was uncovered in late 2022. The fraud led to billions in lost capital, and the company's founder, Sam Bankman-Fried, was found guilty on seven counts of fraud and could face years in prison.[86]

Consumers trusted this exchange to manage their cryptocurrencies—their holdings in Bitcoin, Ethereum, and other currencies. Yet the company engaged in alleged fraud and mismanaged these assets.

The very centralized nature of these exchanges is mainly responsible for the events that transpired and the lack of trust in certain portions of the cryptocurrency ecosystem. However, cryptocurrency and blockchain will succeed due to the decentralized nature of their systems.

There is a hint of irony that large, centralized systems have created conditions for the theft of decentralized assets. It's also worth noting that various collapses have been more closely linked with fraud and deception. Moreover, the Bitcoin ecosystem continues to lack safeguards around regulation.

For these and other reasons, I have never stored Bitcoin in exchanges. Instead, I've stored it in the ledger of the cryptocurrency, as this is the best way right now for me to manage my access and security. In the future, when Web 3.0 fully emerges, users will have greater access to store their digital items and cryptocurrencies on the ledgers that power the underlying Metaverse economy.

Meanwhile, with the advancement of the Metaverse, the United States government and other nations around the globe will need to step forward to establish a framework. The reason is that they will not be able to put this technology back into the bag. Such a framework is essential, as blockchain is vital to the future success of the Metaverse, which will provide an immense boost to the US and global economy.

The Metaverse will not be built by one individual company; it will require individuals to move between various digital environments, from the world of *Fortnite* to others. And it will require that individuals are able to bring their digital items with them. When two different worlds are interoperable, the blockchain can act as a confirmation mechanism to authenticate that a specific user owns an object. When users buy their digital items and store them in a digital wallet, the blockchain on which these wallets operate will provide access and proof of ownership. With blockchain, users can switch between wallets easily. Think of it as moving your money from one traditional bank to another. Switching digital wallets, though, will be even easier.

Looking ahead, digital wallets will provide the critical infrastructure and services that enable the visualization and interfaces for all users. The nature of this encryption across the entirety of cryptocurrency will be essential for it to establish a network effect, increase user adoption, and prevent data breaches or theft of their items.

In addition, the nature of blockchain will allow users to secure their items and protect their transactions. The open and transparent nature of the technology ensures that users can trust these digital worlds and the underlying economy on which they will be built. If a person makes a Metasite and has an open, virtual store that rivals a physical one, it must have a transaction mechanism that enables consumers to buy products and other items.

These transactions must be fast and secure, just as if they had been purchased in the real world. In addition, they must be able to confirm the details of that transaction. The blockchain—which records these transactions—acts as a digital receipt, which holds both the buyer and seller to the terms of their contract.

And their digital wallets will allow users to carry various cryptocurrencies and their digital goods, including accessories for avatars, items for their Metasites, and more.

What else? Well, they can purchase music, movies, games, and more. Wallets may also include secure communications with friends, allowing you to invite them to a special event or plan your adventures in the Metaverse.

Finally, remember that the nature of blockchain will be critical to brands.

As a result, there will likely be deep policy conversations around brands and copyrights in the Metaverse. Brands will rely on blockchain to ensure that they can prevent the pirating of products and services, and the confirmation of blockchain transactions will provide greater security to prevent black-market items.

In summary, blockchains provide six key benefits that will be essential to the Metaverse: security, decentralization, trust, interoperability, smart contracts, and the financial mechanism of cryptocurrency. These will be crucial to boosting the long-term upside for early adopters and the creative developers who bring the Metaverse to the masses.

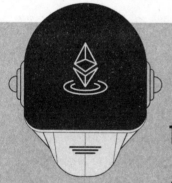

BLOCKCHAINS PROVIDE SIX KEY BENEFITS THAT WILL BE ESSENTIAL TO THE METAVERSE: SECURITY, DECENTRALIZATION, TRUST, INTEROPERABILITY, SMART CONTRACTS, AND THE FINANCIAL MECHANISM OF CRYPTOCURRENCY.

Now, let's look at how to realize economic rewards in the Metaverse.

SCAN ME FOR MORE INFO

CHAPTER 8

"DIGITAL ITEMS": THINK LOYALTY PROGRAMS ON STEROIDS

There are several words people should love to hear.

A child joyfully screaming, "Mommy" or "Daddy."

A friend or spouse saying, "I love you."

Or when a restaurant waiter says, "The owner has picked up the check."

But there may be no sweeter words in business than when an airline customer service representative says, "We've upgraded your seat to first class."

Airline loyalty programs reward frequent fliers with bonuses for using their services regularly. Fly with Delta Air Lines or use its loyalty-based American Express credit card enough and you'll eventually earn Silver Medallion Status.

Then, there's Gold Status. Then Platinum. And Diamond. Each tier provides various rewards and perks, including access to airport lounges, free tickets, upgrades to better seats, and even early access to ticket sales for popular sporting and entertainment events.

Airline loyalty programs have thrived because airlines and customers know that loyalty can pay off. Over the last decade, airline companies built massive marketing campaigns around credit card accounts and free travel. The goal was to entice users to travel exclusively on a specific airline.

Airlines aren't alone in their pursuits.

Retailers from Target to Walmart have loyalty programs designed to bring customers back to their stores. For example, they might offer exclusive member deals or early access to various products before the holiday shopping season. Many spas and hotels provide points-based systems that provide customers with opportunities for free services or upgrades. Starbucks and Chipotle will give you free coffee and food if you buy enough of their products.

One of the great driving forces in today's loyalty-program universe is the interconnection of various brands. Individuals enrolled in Starbucks Rewards and Delta Rewards can earn miles from their coffee purchases. Individuals who use American Express cards can obtain free Uber dollars every month, while Uber users can get access to American Express points. In the future, this interconnectivity won't just apply to big corporations. Anyone will hopefully have the power to co-brand and co-market with other businesses and entrepreneurs in the Metaverse to build loyal audiences.

Reward programs can and will incentivize future consumption—especially among the company's top and most loyal customers. In chapter 4, I talked about the 80/20 principle of business revenue generation. If you're a business owner or entrepreneur, you should recognize that 20 percent of customers are responsible for roughly

80 percent of revenue. And don't forget about the superusers, also known as whales, who are willing to spend big—sometimes ten to twenty times more than the average user. These whales will align their values and beliefs with a brand. They may wish to become a part of the community and should be rewarded for their loyal following.

IN THE FUTURE, THIS INTERCONNECTIVITY WON'T JUST APPLY TO BIG CORPORATIONS. ANYONE WILL HOPEFULLY HAVE THE POWER TO CO-BRAND AND CO-MARKET WITH OTHER BUSINESSES AND ENTREPRENEURS IN THE METAVERSE TO BUILD LOYAL AUDIENCES.

That incentivization sits at the heart of every loyalty program in the business world. When the Metaverse starts to dominate the global business landscape in the decade ahead, maximizing revenue from the top customers will require an even greater effort to reward them through a loyalty program. So, think of today's loyalty programs . . . *on steroids*.

That's what I want to show you right now.

DEFINING LOYALTY

You can generate incredible revenue from your most loyal customers.

That's one reason companies spend so much money managing loyalty programs and marketing to these top customers. According to Fortune Business Insights, the global loyalty management industry totaled $5.29 billion in 2022. That figure is poised to surpass $28 billion by 2030—and the growth of Web 3.0 and the Metaverse can serve as a major influence moving forward.[87]

But let's take a quick step back to understand the initial challenge to overcome when it comes to the Metaverse. First, individual customers' trust is at the center of customer loyalty and personal brand relationships.

Please don't take my word for it.

According to a 2018 Salesforce Research study, "95% of customers are more likely to be loyal to a company they trust." In addition, "92% are more likely to purchase additional products and services from trusted businesses."[88]

But let's consider how trust has evolved in business over the last fifty years.

There was a time when companies would start at the local level, like a mom-and-pop operation that had five to ten physical locations. Perhaps restaurants. Maybe a hardware store. Even grocery stores. Remember, big brands today, like McDonald's, Kroger, or Lowe's, started with several locations and grew into large corporations over time. Those companies didn't succeed because they had deep pockets or employees with master of business administration (MBA) degrees.

Trust was critical from the onset.

From inception, these companies relied on local relationships with customers, banks, partners, and communities. People behind the counter likely knew a lot of the customers' names. Accountability was critical to the company's physical expansion over the years. Any breach of trust might have ended up in the newspaper, courtroom, or center of gossip at the local barber shop. Trust was essential—a cornerstone of success.

In the 1990s, however, the strategy of building trust started to change.

The physical world slowly started to give way to the digital world.

The advent of the internet altered the way customers and companies engaged. Brands could reach far more customers on the internet—from across state lines to worldwide. The digital expansion enabled a once-small online bookstore called Amazon.com to grow into the world leader in e-commerce. But to reach that level, successful digital companies like Amazon had to first establish trust in a new digital commerce ecosystem.

Web 2.0 brought brands closer to consumers than ever before. Today's sites are designed for direct consumption. Any company that builds a business today follows a unique template for developing its online presence.

Their websites almost always seek to establish trust quickly. For example, companies share customer testimonials, product stories, service reviews, and personal stories to help immerse the customer in the brand.

In addition, many sites reward customers for referrals. This strategy is important, as it can become a critical source of new business. The 2018 Salesforce Research survey I noted also found that "93% of customers are more likely to recommend a company they trust."[89]

Of course, trust is earned. Web 2.0 brought nearly two decades of privacy concerns, fueled by digital breaches, hacking events, and stolen customer information. It fueled an intense rise in cybersecurity spending and centralized companies that own and sell customer data to third parties. As a result, it is increasingly common to see websites explicitly note that they will not sell new customer data when requesting sensitive information like email addresses, phone numbers, and more.

Now, we are entering a new world of customer engagement. The Metaverse will turn the Web 2.0 model on its side rather quickly—like what e-commerce did to physical retail over the last twenty years. Today, customers can buy products online, have them shipped to their homes, and then send them back if they're not content with the purchase.

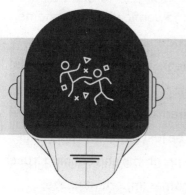

NOW, WE ARE ENTERING A NEW WORLD OF CUSTOMER ENGAGEMENT.

In the Metaverse, customers will directly interact with brands digitally in a way that is foreign to our current ways of doing business. But building trust and loyalty will be difficult initially for some businesses. The reason is simple: this isn't all about the physical world. A customer might be thousands of miles away in physical life but interacting with digital avatars and other actors in the Metaverse. They digitally interact with brands and their products.

This is a different sensory experience—and it requires a completely different approach. People must establish trust to create loyalty in a place where physical handshakes and eye contact aren't the norms.

In addition, customers will largely interact with other avatars, and they'll want to ensure the items they purchase are verified, are unique, and can't be copied. They need to know the people they meet in the Metaverse are who they say they are—which is why technology is so critical to building the trust process.

That said, strong growth in these digital worlds will include reputational factors. This 4D experience will be boundless and require digital trust mechanisms to bring brands and customers together in a way that establishes unprecedented loyalty.

As discussed in previous chapters, blockchain quickly establishes the importance of trust and verification of customer purchases and interactions. And interoperability will help ensure that customers can take their digital items into new digital worlds and across networks.

The bulk of the technology required to make this transition possible exists today. Deploying it will be just part of the challenge. Recognizing the importance of loyalty programs and building trust with customers through rewards is another important phase.

TAKING LOYALTY TO THE METAVERSE

Loyalty and brand relationships change immensely in the digital world, and companies must quickly establish programs that build trust and boost revenue. Airline companies, retail brands, entrepreneurs, and anyone with a product or service should start building these programs immediately. Similarly, excited consumers should seek out their favorite brands' programs that will offer immersive experiences and reward their loyalty.

As we dive deeper into relationships between brands and their customers in the digital world, I will discuss loyalty programs across five important classifications.

The first is through virtual currencies and digital items. Blockchain will allow companies to provide rewards in the form of cryptocurrency and other digital items. This will enable users to use that currency at a brand's store, redeem it for unique rewards, and even access exclusive events and products. For example, in today's world, arcade-style restaurants like Dave & Buster's have their own currency for games at their physical locations, and they provide rewards for users who regularly spend money with the restaurant and its associated arcade games.

As previously mentioned, digital currencies and items like NFTs can be stored in a user's digital wallet on the blockchain. With these digital items, brands can encourage users to regularly visit their Metasites, score exclusive digital merchandise, or do anything else a brand might imagine. These virtual currencies can act as the backbone of loyalty programs much the same way that an airline's miles program encourages the use of its services.

Meanwhile, NFTs are critical due to one fundamental characteristic: NFTs are fraud-proof, as I explored earlier in chapter 3.

Bluntly put, they can't be copied or replicated.

Due to their unique coding and the blockchain, there is only one unique NFT at a time (although they can be a part of a limited-edition series or collection). These digital assets can include art, music, in-game items, and other digital rewards. And because they are interoperable and unique, they are also scarce.

There's one last thing I love about NFTs that will make them even more enticing loyalty products: when customers can link their wallets to their NFTs, these digital items are tradable. By making these items tradable, it opens the entire digital economy to new users and existing users who may want to trade for these items or use them to score upgrades or other rewards.

One of the first companies to dive deeply into NFTs was Marriott, the famous hotel chain. The company commissioned three artists to create NFTs for a Miami art fair. During the fair, users could win these NFTs and two hundred thousand loyalty points to the hotel chain. After the success of this program, Marriott quickly established the launch of NFT loyalty rewards that could be traded among members of the hotel's member programs. Although the program is no longer operating, it was an innovative experiment that linked art with travel and hospitality.[90]

NFTs have also become critical loyalty products for major sports leagues like the National Basketball Association, Major League Baseball, and the National Football League. They've also become an increasingly popular way to attract users to wearable objects in the Metaverse from brands like Burberry, Louis Vuitton, and Kiehl's.

Second, I love the idea of gamification moving forward as a unique way to make users think and engage with new products. For example, in the Metaverse, we've discussed the possibility of Adidas creating lifelike sports simulations on its Metasite.

So, imagine the possibility of users playing games or beating challenges that provide them with cryptocurrency or other rewards. Such immersive experiences could boost brand engagement.

This gamification concept was popular in a digital experience offered on The Sandbox—a Metaverse platform—that centered on rap artist Snoop Dogg. In the experience, users could visit virtual plots of land owned by celebrities. In fact, someone paid $500,000 just to be Snoop Dogg's neighbor in the virtual world called Snoopverse.[91]

Users could also win a party pass to Snoop Dogg's digital mansion. In addition, they could engage in games and other small activities that provided rewards. One NFT even provided one thousand people the exclusive opportunity to hang out with Snoop Dogg's avatar at his virtual mansion.

Third, brands will likely concede their values to the values of the individual. In the Metaverse, trust is built on engagement, interaction, and knowing the customer's likes and dislikes. Through innovative analysis and engagement, brands can get to know their customers and create personalized experiences for their best and most loyal fans in the Metaverse.

THROUGH INNOVATIVE ANALYSIS AND ENGAGEMENT, BRANDS CAN GET TO KNOW THEIR CUSTOMERS AND CREATE PERSONALIZED EXPERIENCES FOR THEIR BEST AND MOST LOYAL FANS IN THE METAVERSE.

Brands will quickly understand—through proper analysis—the types of rewards or products that will entice their top 20 percent of customers to visit and interact with their Metasites.

Remember, this is not necessarily an exercise in trying to market to tens of thousands of people at once. On the contrary, marketing directly to whales—the people who will gladly spend a significant amount of money on a brand—will deepen relationships and heighten their individual experiences in the physical and digital environments.

Fourth, as brands get to know their top users, these Metaverse loyalty programs must expand beyond the digital world. They must give their top customers access to real-world experiences. For example, Adidas might provide tickets to live sports events, while musicians might provide opportunities to attend live shows in their town.

Brands must properly navigate the balance between physical and digital experiences and allow their customers to experience something in the real world they had never imagined.

My fifth and final thought on loyalty programs is that networking is critical for audience-building and partnership potential.

The most loyal fans and customers must have an opportunity to meet each other, create shared experiences, and benefit from their willingness to bring new members to the community. In today's physical marketing world, companies regularly provide financial and social incentives to invite new users to their experiences.

In the Metaverse, this could be a turbocharged marketing experience. Companies will no longer rely on the rules and limitations of the physical world. Instead, rewarding a loyal customer for bringing their friend to a Metasite is as easy as asking both to sign onto their screens and immerse themselves instantly in a brand site—all without ever asking them to leave the house or put on shoes.

The Metaverse will create a new business strategy ahead for loyalty programs. It will alter how customers interact with brands and will produce innovations in how companies get new and existing customers to spend money—which is the subject of our next chapter.

There's a much different model that will make it easier for businesses to find new customers and sell. And it's unlike any customer-generation platform you've seen.

Goodbye, Web 2.0 name generation.

Hello, post-acquisition customer strategies in the Metaverse.

GOODBYE, WEB 2.0 NAME GENERATION. HELLO, POST-ACQUISITION CUSTOMER STRATEGIES IN THE METAVERSE.

SCAN ME FOR MORE INFO

CHAPTER 9

REVENUE SHARE: STOP PRE-PAYING FOR CLICKS AND START POST-PAYING FOR CUSTOMERS

Economists track 190 nations and measure their gross domestic product (GDP), a figure that represents the size of nations' economic output. It measures consumer spending, government spending, business investment, and the difference between imports and exports. It's a significant figure as it helps us understand the size and influence of a nation's economic might. Just sixteen countries have GDPs north of $1 trillion per year. By basic deduction, 174 countries have a GDP below $1 trillion. Therefore, 174 countries could have GDPs that are less than the projected value of the global online advertising industry in 2027. That's right. Online marketing could reach $1.08 trillion within the next few years, according to Allied Market Research.[92]

The internet's marketing ecosystem is a behemoth, largely cornered by large search companies, social media giants, and entities exploiting consumer data to extract every dollar possible. Centralized players continue to operate what resembles something closer to a digital oligarchy or online feudalism than a free economic system.

Let's look at the existing digital advertising space and where I think dramatic changes can occur in the next rendition of the internet, the Metaverse.

ADVERTISING IN THE METAVERSE

If you've ever run a business online, you know there are plenty of options for advertising products or services. In today's digital environment, three marketing models dominate the advertising landscape. These strategies are how most content creators and businesses drive traffic to their sites.

Each typically requires businesses to pre-pay for all traffic.

These models are PPC (Pay Per Click), PPM (Pay Per Impression), and PPA (Pay Per Action). Companies pay a fee for each time their ads are clicked, are displayed, or produce a sale, respectively.

Pay-per-click (PPC) advertising is exactly as it sounds.

If you run your business, you pay a marketer only when someone clicks the advertisement. This has succeeded in today's environment mainly because it's a highly targeted marketing strategy.

Given that marketers have a deep knowledge of the people they are marketing to, companies can advertise directly to individuals based on location, demographics, and other vital factors. I'll soon discuss the importance of maintaining and controlling your data in the future, because data is the lifeblood of today's digital marketing landscape.

By paying only when someone clicks an ad, a company can easily measure its return on investment (ROI) for paid links. The conversion rate is based on the number of people who purchase something divided by the number of people who click the link.

Many companies like the PPC model because it's easy to budget, provides good performance data around messaging, and can deliver quick results. Plus, advertisers can deploy PPC campaigns very fast.

However, PPC can be very expensive across various sectors.

PPC is largely based on specific keywords tracked in search engines—and key players like Google and Microsoft control the practice.

Companies might pay hefty fees in highly competitive markets to own specific keywords that will generate consumer interest. For example, in 2021, Google AdWords charged significant sums for various keywords for a business to appear in the top searches on the engine. According to CNBC, Google generated $147 billion in 2020 from its search, video, and display advertising.[93]

WordStream notes that the term *insurance* costs businesses $54.91 per click, while the search term *loans* costs $44.28 per click.[94]

Meanwhile, in 2021, the search phrase *best car insurance in North Carolina* cost companies an eye-popping $220 per click, according to PPC Hero.[95]

In addition, there are instances of click fraud. For example, imagine you and a competitor are fighting over the same keyword. What stops them from repeatedly clicking on your links and costing you a small fortune? In 2006, Google settled a $90 million click-fraud class action lawsuit brought by online retailers. At that time, Google generated $6.14 billion in revenue.[96] Today, it generates more than $282 billion.[97] That $90 million lawsuit didn't make a dent in Google's profits.

While today's PPC campaigns typically employ false-click detection, it's worth noting that there is very little control in this process for the advertiser.

Next, let's talk about pay-per-impression (PPM) advertising.

In this case, companies pay a flat fee for every one thousand impressions. Think of this advertising as carpet-bombing the internet with banner ads, lines, and other eye-grabbing messages. However, this strategy is less targeted and aims to replicate the mass-marketing strategy of different media like television and newspapers.

While PPM is very cost-effective, the less-targeted strategy fails to provide companies with adequate measurements. In addition, the success or failure of a campaign can be random, meaning it may take time to replicate the response, and this model can be quite complicated, largely due to costs. Business owners will therefore need to budget in advance. They also need to ensure they have cash, or they'll need to put these costs on a credit card without any certainty that it will create new revenue.

Finally, companies might consider pay-per-action (PPA) or pay-per-buy.

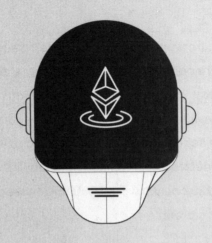

DATA IS THE LIFEBLOOD OF TODAY'S DIGITAL MARKETING LANDSCAPE.

In this case, a company might advertise on a social media site, a website, or other places. That company might pay if a customer clicks a link that takes someone to a specific website, makes a purchase, or provides information.

This is one of the most advanced and targeted models today, but not every advertising company wants to do the heavy lifting. Many online ad networks would prefer to collect smaller, more reliable revenue streams than pay based on one or two large purchases.

Naturally, most companies must rely on advertising on Google or Facebook and pay for clicks, hoping that the clicks will turn into customers. Unfortunately, this reliance might cause companies to lack complete control or certainty of advertising campaigns, affecting their cash flow.

Today's largest search marketing and social media companies have largely cornered the current digital advertising market. Want to reach the widest audience possible? You can't just set up a web page, publicize a blog, and hope that potential customers will just find you.

In today's competitive e-commerce environment, Facebook and Google (alongside marketing affiliate companies like Mediavine and AdSense) monetize a company's desire for business by selling priority within search results and monetizing traffic to a specific webpage or commerce channel.

In the Metaverse, however, companies can use a much better model to generate new business, maximize revenue, and expand audience potential. Brands and consumers can also engage across multiple networks. Whether it's Web 2.0 or the future Metaverse, attracting news audiences will be essential. The process of introducing customers to new brands will be an important marketing practice that produces new revenue for all participants.

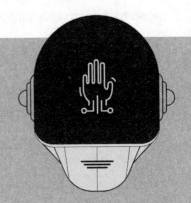

THE PROCESS OF INTRODUCING CUSTOMERS TO NEW BRANDS WILL BE AN IMPORTANT MARKETING PRACTICE THAT PRODUCES NEW REVENUE FOR ALL PARTICIPANTS.

To boost that potential revenue, I want to share with you an engaging model for business and customer relationships called a *revenue share*.

Of course, many people already know the business term. A revenue share is a simple agreement between two parties. Under the terms, a business partner receives a percentage of a company's revenue from selling another company's product or service. On the surface, this may resemble a cost-per-acquisition model, but it's a little deeper than this.

Instead of going through a third-party marketer, partners will provide marketing, advertising, and lead generation and refer their existing customers to another business. In addition, there is a critical word-of-mouth component because a partner is largely acting on behalf of the other company.

When setting up these relationships, parties must establish clear guidelines. This includes insight into how much each brand contributes to a new lead and the touchpoints and engagements of all users. It can be quite difficult to determine an accurate breakdown of each cost and the value of each transaction. In addition, it can be hard to quantify purchase decisions and the psychology of each customer.

That said, parties should agree on specific percentages and financial metrics to optimize the relationship and value of the lead. Loyal customers who believe in a brand that becomes a partner will increase their general trust and willingness to try something referred to them. Under terms of a revenue share, a partner will receive a predetermined amount of money after each transaction.

There are plenty of benefits to revenue shares. Primarily, they allow a company to access a partner's customer base, marketing knowledge, and even advertising resources. In addition, these agreements can create some synergy and alignment in the two companies' businesses. Those are in the real world.

When we move into the Metaverse, the agreements are a little different, as the technology offers trust, verification, and unlimited potential that is unlike anything we've witnessed in economic history.

In the Metaverse, revenue share agreements are already common.

For example, in 2021, Nike partnered with the virtual platform *Roblox*. Nike, a global apparel brand powerhouse, released a limited-edition virtual sneaker. Players could buy these sneakers for their *Roblox* avatars, and the digital Items were exclusive.

Under the terms of the agreement, both companies split the revenue. In addition, the two companies created a popular virtual experience called the "Nike Game Room" that allowed users to compete in a virtual obstacle course. Nike provided the obstacle course, while *Roblox* provided the audience.

This is just one small example of a Metaverse revenue share.

But there are plenty of other opportunities in the Metaverse.

Developers of Metaverse projects could work with companies to boost in-game purchases, advertising opportunities, and digital items as well as increase new revenue channels. For example, in the Metaverse's vast real estate market, companies might purchase virtual land and develop Metasites, virtual experiences, and storefronts to build revenue opportunities.

These developers might provide capital to metaverse platforms like The Sandbox or Decentraland in the future. Revenue shares might also include the sale of virtual goods. Creators might need developers to help create virtual items like clothing, skins, and other digital goods that can be stored safely in one's digital wallet.

Revenue shares might also include virtual events. For example, if someone can help sell tickets to a virtual concert or event, they can receive direct payment for their contributions.

Finally, we may also see new licensing agreements allowing individuals to use various technologies and assets to develop their Metaverse projects.

The revenue share model will be critical moving forward.

But before we discuss how it can adequately be implemented, I want to discuss revenue share at the executive level. Revenue share models can be more attractive than the traditional venture capital or investment model. Typically, we see many investors demand equity and a percentage of profits linked to the long-term viability of a business.

Currently, Meta owns a virtual platform called Horizon Worlds. In 2022, Meta announced that it would create a revenue share model for developers in this universe. The fee: Meta demands 47.5 percent of all revenue, which includes a 30 percent hardware platform fee. In addition, the company also requires hefty fees for in-world purchases and a 17.5 percent cut for Horizon Worlds, according to 9to5Mac.[98]

For example, if someone sells an item for $1.00, Meta commands a $0.30 fee. Meanwhile, the platform fee is $0.17 for Horizon Worlds. The creator will walk away—before taxes—with $0.53.

Huge fees are to be expected. Meta Platforms had previously planned to spend billions on the development of its platform, with allocations that would reach upward of $250 billion over a decade. However, these projects have been scaled down due to investor pushback.

The fees are interesting not only because of their size but also because CEO Mark Zuckerberg had previously criticized revenue shares of other large technology companies. His critiques included remarks about the 30 percent revenue share agreement between Apple and its developers. Zuckerberg had previously promised that developers on Meta's projects would "keep all the money they earn (minus taxes)."[99]

I envision something far more collaborative and democratic than the model presented by Meta Platforms. Let me dive deeper into my preferred revenue share model in the future Metaverse.

INNOVATING IN THE METAVERSE WITH BLOCKCHAIN

As I noted, blockchain technology is central to the Metaverse's potential.

No longer will users need to sign agreements up front or pre-pay for advertising. Instead, agreements will compensate partners on the backside of a transaction.

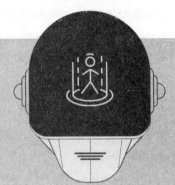

BLOCKCHAIN TECHNOLOGY IS CENTRAL TO THE METAVERSE'S POTENTIAL.

Through basic referral marketing, we can directly track inter-actions on the blockchain and confirm the traffic directed to companies. In addition, these agreements don't just last a series of days; they can last in perpetuity.

Consider how this could serve as a dramatic overhaul of the digital advertising space. We're talking about trillions of dollars potentially shifting from traditional online marketing practices to referral-based systems that can track and compensate partners instantly through blockchain and direct payments.

Thanks to blockchain, these agreements are fully transparent and visible to anyone. Partners can have one contract, or they can develop large contracts around specific content that divide revenue and expand across the Metaverse like tentacles of an octopus, developing new deals that deliver payments and coordinate new partnerships and new financial streams.

Contracts can begin with a fifty-fifty split between two parties. Then, as new developers and content producers join, they can quickly be added to the individual block that tracks total revenue and contractually divides it.

Over time, a content project, a Metasite, and a virtual concert series could have five partners generating various percentages.

These events can expand wider, establishing reliable, contractual sources of money.

I'm not discussing a revenue share model where companies pay platform developers. Rather, I'm talking about the ability for people to make real money by directing traffic to businesses in real time and ensuring their cut. So, if you have a marketing list today, all individuals who purchase a product directly from another company would quickly compensate you on the back end of the transaction.

Instead of paying for marketing lists that might be incomplete, paying a major advertising giant like Facebook or AdSense, or engaging in fading marketing practices that lack measurability, you can pay referrals once revenue has been received. This business model is ideal for start-ups, entrepreneurs, and other companies that might not have much money to start and can't afford to incur up front costs. See how this process could quickly overhaul a global marketing business?

But it goes beyond just simple marketing. The perpetuity of this action is unique. Instead of creating a one-off transaction with a one-off referral, the revenue-sharing model can create a gamifi-cation environment.

Imagine if you referred someone to have a meal at a nearby restaurant. And then, every time they went to that restaurant for the rest of their lives, *you* would receive a few cents on the transactions.

You would receive a direct payment every time because you participated in the revenue share. And every time they swipe their credit card at the restaurant, the transaction and your referral are registered on the blockchain, guaranteeing your payments.

Combining this transaction model with digital items will also accelerate the relationship between the specific customer and the restaurant. For example, the restaurant could send a custom offer directly to that customer in the form of an NFT that includes discounts for the items they purchase the most. And within that offer—tracked on the blockchain—is a line of code that states you, the referrer, receive a share of the revenue each time that customer visits the restaurant.

Now, apply this to every restaurant in the town.

Every shopping center and every store in the mall.

Apply it to the universal potential of the Metaverse and the opportunity for creatives to help develop NFTs, custom offers, and unlimited revenue—a few cents or dollars at a time—that compounds and grows. It could result in an endless well of capital spurred through your audiences and their trust in you.

The process starts at the very beginning of development in the Metaverse. Companies that open Metaverse businesses should work with artists and developers up front. But instead of paying these artists and creatives for one-off payments, the longevity of projects and sales on Metasites can also last in perpetuity. This is why I'm focused on the Metaverse and the development of digital items and projects that can be widely distributed. As developers, we can agree on a revenue share and find new partners who will help establish new relationships in the future.

This is a radical departure from the way things are and have been.

And it is a move toward the way things should be.

CHAPTER 10

WHOEVER OWNS YOUR DATA OWNS YOUR WORLD

Put a video on YouTube.

Post a song on Spotify.

Publish a blog post on a centralized content platform like Medium.

The immediate problem for such creators is that they have little access to and knowledge of who their top readers or viewers are.

That's the nature of today's digital commerce world.

This makes it challenging to run a business through a centralized media platform. What's worse, if you sell on a website like Amazon, not only will the e-commerce giant control the customer data, but it'll also control payments made to you—for two to four weeks.[100]

Today, the customer and the creator totally depend on the centralized platform. You can't directly market to your fan base. And if you're a fan, it's even more difficult to interact directly with your favorite brands.

Why is this?

Look at the state of the e-commerce world and the problems related to data privacy in today's economy, and you'll realize that data isn't safe in most people's hands.

In 2022, the average cost of a data breach increased to $4.35 million, according to legal firm Morgan Lewis.[101] That might not seem like much money to a big technology company like Amazon or Google, but it's a massive amount of money for a small business.

Unfortunately, in today's economy, people tend to think their data is primarily controlled by Silicon Valley giants. However, consumer data is actually stored in many computers of small businesses across the country. Local businesses collect sales data in their files, check in with customers, and always look for new business. In addition, local charities hold donor credit card numbers for recurring donations.

When I say your data is everywhere, I'm not just talking about Facebook or your email account. There are plenty of places that hackers can exploit. For example, the most common victims of ransomware attacks are small businesses across the United States.[102] In this case, a hacker attacks a small business, freezes its computers, and demands a ransom for the files to be unlocked. If a company can't pay, it'll lose mountains of customer information necessary for its business to operate. And even if the company does pay, the data has been compromised.

As a result, the relationship between the customer and the company can be severely damaged.

Most people associate large data breaches with hacking events at Experian or Target. Unfortunately, the truth is that your data isn't very safe anywhere in today's tech environment. For

YOUR DATA ISN'T VERY SAFE ANYWHERE IN TODAY'S TECH ENVIROMENT.

example, you likely don't think about your data security when you're rushed into the emergency room, but you probably should. *U.S. News & World Report* notes that ransomware attacks on hospitals doubled between 2016 and 2023.[103]

Fortunately, that will change.

In the Metaverse, the technology that backs individual transactions will promote transparency, accountability, and privacy. And with that integration, creatives and content producers can directly engage their audiences without the need for Amazon's centralized systems or to pay for promotions through YouTube, Spotify, or the dozens of television streaming services.

Take a breath and think about that for a moment.

The idea is that your information will be safe for once. More importantly, you will be able to own and control your data for the first time in this massive digital economy—and so will your customers.

In today's digital world, consumers are mainly at the mercy of Silicon Valley tech giants. Companies like Amazon, Spotify, and Alphabet collect and store incredible amounts of personal data on their servers.

This data is critical to their business models.

What sort of data is collected? Information about your internet search history, your payment methods, the music you streamed, the shows you've watched, the videos you watched on YouTube, your location data, your purchase history, the types of ads you've clicked, and the products that you didn't want to buy.

These servers might know you better than some of your friends. Businesses use this data to determine customer likes and dislikes.

For example, if you ordered a yoga mat on Amazon, you might be likely to purchase athletic apparel the next time you go to a yoga studio to practice ... and you'll eventually receive a marketing message about some.

Have you ever felt like your computer is listening to you and advertising to you directly? Most likely, these companies are operating on your previous search history and sending you advertising around potential products or services you might want to purchase.

There are several core problems around data management today.

The primary criticism centers on targeted advertising when it comes to third-party access. Data collection and analysis are central to third-party companies' business models.

They use targeted advertising to sell products based on customer profiles constructed from your data. Naturally, this creates many questions about personal data and privacy. Should these companies be able to collect all this data? And who should own it? Most Americans don't know about the somewhat shady business practices of data brokerages. These third-party companies collect personal information from the public and sell it or license the data for profit. If you search your name on Google, for example, you'll likely find a site like Spokeo, which has your name, address, location, and phone numbers. And it's all for sale.

In 2021, roughly four thousand data brokerages were operating in an industry worth $200 billion.[104] This is a largely secretive business. In fact, in 2019, the United States Senate held a hearing on data brokerages to consider possible regulation.[105] However, the data brokers who were invited to the hearing didn't show up.

These brokers collect everything about a person's digital identity, build profiles of individuals, and then sell or license this information to third parties. Buyers can include parties like car dealerships looking to sell new vehicles or even foreign governments looking to spy on Americans. In 2021, former Deputy National Security Advisor Matthew Pottinger warned the Senate Intelligence Committee about data availability through brokerages. Pottinger said China had stolen enough personal data to create a dossier on every American over eighteen years old.[106]

It goes without saying that if a product is free on the internet or in an app, the actual product is probably *you*. Companies collect information and sell it to third parties. If you've ever downloaded an app that provides a free flashlight for your phone, consider why that application asks to share your location data before you can turn the flashlight on.

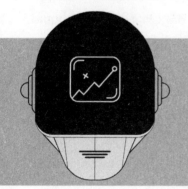

IT GOES WITHOUT SAYING THAT IF A PRODUCT IS FREE ON THE INTERNET OR IN AN APP, THE ACTUAL PRODUCT IS PROBABLY *YOU*.

Again, you're the product. And, if you're a business owner, so are your customers.

The second major problem with data management today is the lack of transparency. It's not evident how these companies collect and store data.

Naturally, individuals should raise concerns about the security of their most vulnerable data. They should feel nervous about the stability and safety of their data, which is increasingly susceptible to large breaches.

Companies will collect data for various business purposes. These practices fuel questions about the safety and security of this data. In addition, it is evident how little control most consumers have over their own personal data.

Let's investigate several of the largest data aggregators on the planet.

We'll start with Apple, the largest consumer-facing technology company in the world. Perhaps you know Apple as a company that sells iPhones, iPads, Mac computers, and other hardware. It has also dramatically ramped up its services business in recent years with Apple Music and its very popular App Store.

The company doesn't use customer data to sell you products directly. It does use the data as a tool to reengineer its products. For example, the company will monitor your computer activity to better understand how you use a device or specific software. When problems arise, your device will "phone home," sending a message to the company to inform it of a glitch or way to improve. This isn't very interesting in the world of data privacy, but it involves significant levels of trust and transparency.

The company will also use your music history to make a specific recommendation in its App Store. For example, it might suggest a new song in Apple Music based on your previous playlist. And it might learn your preferences with its AI-powered assistant, Siri, to better answer your questions and follow prompts and future commands. Again, your data is critical to the functionality. In addition, it may use your data to create personalized advertisements catered to your tastes and consumption history.

Finally, it's worth noting that the company will also use consumer data to verify payment information, prevent fraud, and ensure the security of devices and personal identities. Consumer data is central to these mechanisms, and all your data fuels these practices that are vital to the core of the company's business model.

Let's look at a different company. Many people know of the social media platform TikTok, which allows users to create and share videos. TikTok will collect everything—from a user's location and video history to their device type and preferences. All this information is passed along to the Chinese company ByteDance, which owns TikTok.

ByteDance uses this data to enhance its services, provide advertisements, and customize user experiences. However, TikTok has spurred significant concerns about the data privacy of America, given its links to the Chinese Communist Party.[107] As a result, the US government has banned federal employees from using TikTok on government-owned devices like phones and computers. The United States Senate has also held hearings with proposals to outright ban TikTok in the US.

Now, let's look at Spotify—one of the world's largest music streaming platforms. Similarly to Apple and TikTok, Spotify collects user data like location, device type, and music tastes. And, as is the case with most companies, people worry that users don't have enough information on Spotify's marketing practices. What is the company doing with all the user data it's collecting, and what is it doing to keep it safe?

While the safety and security of personal data is required as part of most companies' business models, self-policing can go only so far. The US government, therefore, has attempted to advocate for consumer and data privacy. The Federal Trade Commission (FTC) has fined technology companies like Google, including a $22.5 million fine for bypassing the privacy settings of Apple's Safari browser.[108] The agency also fined Facebook $5 billion for a 2012 scandal in which the social media company collected information without the consent of its users.[109]

On the other side of the Atlantic Ocean, the European Union (EU) has been far stricter in its efforts than the US government. For example, the EU's General Data Protection Regulation (GDPR) of 2018 gave users more control over their data and how it is collected. This regulation applies to all organizations operating within the European block, regardless of location. In addition, the GDPR fines companies for noncompliance.

The EU also slapped Facebook with a €110 million fine in July 2020 for misleading regulators during its approval process for the 2014 acquisition of rival WhatsApp.[110]

In today's environment of data breaches and insecurity, we must look forward to a world that doesn't require government overreach or trust in companies with little incentive to prevent data mismanagement. Even in the early stages of its development, the Metaverse will give users stronger control over their data. Blockchain technology and decentralization can provide security and transparency to digital assets and personal data.

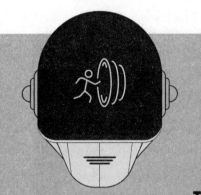

IN TODAY'S ENVIRONMENT OF DATA BREACHES AND INSECURITY, WE MUST LOOK FORWARD TO A WORLD THAT DOESN'T REQUIRE GOVERNMENT OVERREACH OR TRUST IN COMPANIES WITH LITTLE INCENTIVE TO PREVENT DATA MISMANAGEMENT.

The basic truth is that providers don't need a significant amount of their top users' data. They simply need the mechanism to meet them, create with them, engage them, and provide them with unique experiences. And technology can provide you with those opportunities without needing a middleman like Google, Apple, or Meta Platforms.

PRIVACY IN THE METAVERSE

Do you know who your best fans are? It's unlikely if you're posting on YouTube, TikTok, Spotify, or Facebook. Going forward, in the Metaverse, you will control your data because you will essentially be your own studio or publishing company. You will know who your fans, readers, listeners, and viewers are, and you will be able to communicate directly with them and market to them without any intermediary controlling your destiny.

The basic element of personal identity sits at the heart of the Metaverse, blockchain, and other Web 3.0 applications. Digital wallets serve as a tool to store cryptocurrencies and NFTs. These wallets go beyond just managing the digital items that exist; they will carry the digital identity of a person—one that provides unique data about a person's preferences and activities. At the core of these wallets is a concept known as self-sovereign identity. They give people control over their information—and allow them to prove who they are when visiting new websites, engaging with brands, and using applications on their devices.

In the Metaverse, there are several ways that users will be able to better manage and own their data. First, blockchain technology will better promote decentralization and make it harder for a centralized player like Google or a data broker to access and aggregate user data. Within the blockchain, users should have better access and insight into the shared information and the parties it was shared with. Plus, the decentralized nature of this technology will allow users to deny access to individuals or parties outside their networks.

Second, the interoperability of blockchain technologies will make it easier for users to transfer their data and identities from one platform to the next without interruption. When someone leaves the Metaverse entirely, they will take their data and digital tools with them.

The third benefit is the nature of cryptography and the blockchain. As noted, the blockchain operates on a network of nodes; there is no central authority that maintains the data set. This decentralized nature ensures data protection by eliminating aggregation sites. As I noted in a previous chapter, the blockchain makes it possible for smarter, secure contracts, encryption, and digital signatures that keep information safe and confidential.

What does this mean? It means that companies will shift away from the traditional marketing practices of Web 2.0 and mass marketing practices like Pay Per Click (PPC). Instead, companies and content producers will find incentives to build one-on-one relationships that capitalize on the underlying technology.

For example, instead of small businesses running Facebook or Google PPC ads, they can engage customers directly with NFTs. These NFTs—sent directly to users via their digital wallets—could be simple contracts that offer exclusive deals or discounts.

This not only creates an exclusive offer directly for that customer but also creates a situation that prioritizes the privacy of a transaction. Moreover, this strategy aligns perfectly with the current desires of customers. According to consultancy McKinsey & Company, 71 percent of customers want personalized experiences offered by companies. In addition, in my opinion, a large percentage, let's say 66 percent, of customers would be happy to share their data or would consider sharing data if they got something of value in return.[111] The consultancy also notes that even more consumers would be willing to share their data if a company articulates a "clear, compelling value proposition."[112]

This shifts the attention to the most important strategy around marketing: retention. In the Metaverse, retention marketing not only will be the most important strategy to engage customers but will also serve as the highest source of revenue. Again, the top 20 percent of customers should produce at least 80 percent of the revenue.

IN THE METAVERSE, RETENTION MARKETING NOT ONLY WILL BE THE MOST IMPORTANT STRATEGY TO ENGAGE CUSTOMERS BUT WILL ALSO SERVE AS THE HIGHEST SOURCE OF REVENUE.

According to Harvard Business School, increasing retention by 5 percent can increase profitability by 25 percent to 95 percent.[113] Moving forward, the Metaverse will provide companies with an advanced source of retention and higher profits, aided by next-generation tools like NFTs that can and will create personalized experiences.

SCAN ME FOR MORE INFO

CHAPTER 11

HOW XSOLLA INVESTS IN VIDEO GAMES

Silicon Valley sits forty-five minutes southeast of San Francisco, on the outskirts of San Jose, California. It's the nexus of a global venture capital (VC) industry worth nearly $210 billion in 2022.[114]

This industry will grow by nearly 22 percent annually through 2028, according to IMARC Group.[115] That growth trend would put global venture capital assets at more than $708 billion as investors seek greater capital returns outside traditional stock and bond markets.

If you're an entrepreneur or developer with a vision, a product, and a pitch deck, Silicon Valley will quickly become one of your first destination goals for securing funding. There you'll find early investors in some of the world's top technology organizations. Pick any major technology name that dominates today's e-commerce or digital landscape, and it likely found some of its most critical, early investors in these private equity offices.

For example, Draper Associates tapped into electric vehicle giant Tesla and video-gaming platform Twitch in the companies' early days. Marc Lowell Andreessen helped kick-start Twitter and Instagram. Peter Thiel's Founders Fund invested early in Facebook,

Airbnb, and SpaceX. And household names like Adobe, Alphabet, Apple, Cisco, eBay, Intel, LinkedIn, NVIDIA, PayPal, and Zoom also started by raising capital in Silicon Valley.

Venture capitalists will buy into a big idea and work with an entrepreneur through the business plan and the investment. I explored venture capital for a long time and even considered heading down that path with my career. However, I could never really get past the ideas. I love entrepreneurs and big ideas (especially investing in them).

But venture capital requires more than investing and promoting an idea. Venture capitalists manage a portfolio of different early to mid-stage companies. They work diligently on each idea. The process is very time intensive. These managers might serve as board members of their portfolio companies, help manage strategy at the executive level, and mentor the start-up teams.

They do so for one obvious reason: they want to make a lot of money on start-ups.

> **I LOVE IDEAS AND GIVING DEVELOPERS THE TOOLS THEY NEED TO SOLVE BUSINESS PROBLEMS AND GROW THEIR COMPANIES OR PROJECTS. IT'S ESSENTIAL TO PLAY TO YOUR STRENGTHS AND DIRECT ALL YOUR ATTENTION TO WHERE YOUR SKILL SET LIES.**

I've never believed that managing large teams and a dozen investments in start-ups would be my best strength. I love ideas and giving developers the tools they need to solve business problems and grow their companies or projects. It's essential to play to your strengths and direct all your attention to where your skill set lies.

THE VC AND VIDEO GAME INVESTMENT QUESTION

While I'm not interested in running a venture capital fund, I was initially surprised by how little attention the venture capital space pays to the video gaming industry. Since arriving in Los Angeles, I've taken a different path than venture capital managers. I started my own business and created a model that deviates from VC, empowering creators through unique revenue share opportunities. I also thank them because they have given Xsolla many opportunities to grow rapidly and help the video gaming industry expand without significant micromanagement.

But think for a moment.

Why on earth would venture capitalists not be pouring money into video games?

As I've mentioned, video games support a $200 billion industry. They're a core driver of almost every major technology that built the infrastructure behind today's most advanced digital companies. For example, recall that NVIDIA made the chips necessary to fuel the rapid growth of networking on which the video game industry relies. Consumers regularly buy new computers each year to play games, and those games drive more advanced networking and computing capabilities. Mobile games alone are a $100 billion industry, and the cloud-based systems (central to so many technology companies backed by Silicon Valley) not only make this industry's future growth possible but also create the bedrock for the Metaverse and bleeding-edge tech.

Yet venture capitalists barely invest in video games.

There are roughly forty funds engaged in the space (out of more than 1,800 in the US and nearly 3,000 globally). And these funds invest a paltry $50 million each in their gaming portfolios. In addition, most games that receive investment from VC shops largely consist of late-stage games with limited financial upside compared to a game in early-stage development. With these investments, the publishing deals are largely signed, and the games are likely in the mid to final stages of development.

THE POTENTIAL IS PRESENT

According to my calculations, there will be just $2 billion invested in 2023 in a gaming industry that will generate between $470 billion and $530 billion annually by 2030. So, what on earth is happening? Do venture capitalists not understand how games work or this potential market size? Do they think gaming is only for children? Do they not understand that three billion people play video games worldwide and superusers will spend incredible amounts of money in the space?

I imagine they see the potential—largely in an industry that sees business in dollars and cents and profits and losses. I believe the nature of venture capital management practices and how VC firms value businesses are major deterrents to investment.

I'll spare you a long MBA course on valuation, but let's cover a few terms that are tossed out when assigning a monetary value to a company. *Enterprise Value* (EV) refers to a company's combined debt and capital, or all the money it can put to work, while *EBITDA* refers to a company's earnings before interest, tax, depreciation, and amortization. Other times, *EBIT*, or earnings before interest and tax, may be used.

Sometimes, investors will tap into a company because they believe the sum of the company's parts is worth more than the current market capitalization (the number of shares outstanding multiplied by the share prices—regardless of whether it's public or private).

There are many ways to value an investment. In Silicon Valley, when talking about technology investment, we're typically focused on companies still in the early development phase. As a result, their balance sheets will show that they aren't making more money than they are spending, meaning they aren't turning a profit.

Again, these companies are just starting up, building their business, finding new customers, and reinvesting their profits back into the business to grow and expand. Because they aren't profitable, investors don't measure their share price or value compared to their annual profits (a typical Wall Street metric called *Price-to-Earnings Ratio*).

Instead, many VC firms will determine a start-up's value based on its revenues. Further, they will determine the value based on a multiple or price to its current revenue levels, which projects future growth potential. Venture capitalists aren't necessarily worried about profits at that stage of business development. Instead, they want growth—and revenue (measured by quarterly and annual increases or decreases) is the purest measure.

> **VENTURE CAPITALISTS AREN'T NECESSARILY WORRIED ABOUT PROFITS AT THAT STAGE OF BUSINESS DEVELOPMENT. INSTEAD, THEY WANT GROWTH—AND REVENUE (MEASURED BY QUARTERLY AND ANNUAL INCREASES OR DECREASES) IS THE PUREST MEASURE.**

As companies grow, they will likely need to obtain additional capital from other venture capital firms or even private equity companies that want to invest in the potential upside. These companies will hold investment rounds that raise more money at a higher multiple if their growth projections continue—and invite new participants to pledge capital. As a result, some high-growth companies will have multiple investment rounds at increasingly higher valuations.

Typically, the goal is to bring these companies public through an Initial Public Offering (IPO). Then, when the company is listed on a public stock exchange like the New York Stock Exchange (NYSE) or NASDAQ, retail investors can purchase stock and invest in the company.

Traditionally, only accredited investors—individuals who make more than $200,000 annually, or $300,000 for a joint income, or have a net worth above $1 million (less the value of their primary residence)—can invest through alternative investment strategies like venture capital, private equity, or hedge funds.[116] The cost of investing in one of these funds is determined by the fund manager, and investors who apply to invest may be subject to questionnaires about their total assets and other verification.

When a company goes public, it may receive more scrutiny around its profit potential in the future. That said, 2023 trends have been highly difficult for the venture capital industry. Following industry reports provided by investment bankers that we have access to, the number of closings (investments) in the fourth quarter of 2022 and the first quarter of 2023 was the lowest it's been in fifteen years, on par with the wake of the Great Financial Crisis of 2008–2009.

In addition, the industry experienced a black eye with the collapse of Silicon Valley Bank, a major financial institution that provided banking services to many VC firms. Rising interest rates not only reduced access to capital among start-up founders but also impacted the balance sheet of Silicon Valley Bank. The financial institution had invested consumer deposits into long-dated US treasury bonds. As interest rates rose, the value of these bonds declined so much that the institution was technically insolvent. When customers in the VC space started to demand their deposits (largely due to many companies keeping more money in their accounts than the FDIC insures), there was a run on the bank. The bank collapsed in March 2023. It was the second-largest bank failure in US history.

Yet, at the VC stage, growth provides a pathway to higher valuations, and in some cases, you might hear about a company raising money at a private valuation of twenty, thirty, and even forty times revenue. These companies tend to be in high-growth industries such as cryptocurrency and blockchain solutions, healthcare, social networking, or next-generation technologies.

The video game space, however, doesn't tend to generate those types of multiples.

Occasionally, I'll see a video game reach a valuation of three to five times its annual revenue. Unfortunately, that sort of multiple won't attract the attention of many Silicon Valley managers.

And since only about $2 billion was invested in the video game space in 2022, according to my calculations, it makes it even harder for producers to acquire capital through the traditional markets.

Video game companies are not any different than other businesses at the fundamental level. If I pulled case studies from business schools, almost every single company faces one or all of the following challenges:

How can the company sell more products?

How can the company obtain new customers?

How can the company attract new capital?

Venture capitalists excel in helping their portfolio companies not just answer these questions but also create an action plan for achieving the desired results.

But I'm not interested in the venture capital approach. Instead, I think the video game industry has the potential to streamline a lot of the solutions to these questions. I don't think video game publishers need someone to stand over their shoulders and tell them what to do, how to design the game, or how to succeed.

We've seen many incredible video games evolve from nowhere over the last few years. These games didn't require the involvement of financial managers or strategic consultants. I've seen twenty people develop a game and turn it into a $500 million hit; however, venture capital firms will still stand clear of the sector.

I see a unique opportunity in a very high-growth business, with countless potential customers and many people who will want to invest in companies (alongside Xsolla) as we build fundraising platforms.

So, before I dive into how and why Xsolla invests in video games, I want to provide you with the answer to a burning industry question: What does it take to make a *successful* video game?

WHAT SUCCESS LOOKS LIKE—AND HOW TO ENSURE IT

I've thought long and hard about this answer because Xsolla is an investor in the video game industry.

The first "must-have" component of a successful video game centers on the mechanics. The mechanics are the innovation in the game, something that has been achieved and that might have evolved alongside new technology. In many ways, it doesn't matter what the game looks like.

The graphics might be raw in the first iteration, but that doesn't matter—the mechanics and gameplay will draw interest in the game instead. That cognitive interest in how someone plays the game is critical; because if no one understands how to play it, the game simply can't succeed.

The second element of a successful game is the content. We like games with a creative story, but that's not always necessary. If we think back, games like *DOOM*, *Fortnite*, and *Minecraft* originally operated around simple visuals, functionality, and soundtracks.

Those things are largely budgetary and can be resolved with investment.

Even if you're just starting with a simple gameplay, if the story is compelling, it can develop something that captures an audience's imagination. This is why I encourage developers to think about how the game draws players into the story—and how that story can be told by players and influencers who will bring it to the attention of the masses.

The third part of a winning video game is even more essential than the previous two. It's the business component of the game—or what I call the business engine—that will help a game producer distribute the game to the broadest audience possible.

The business engine identifies the right partnerships and influencers to make the game a phenomenon. This process must start right at the onset of development, ensuring that the moment the game has been finished, it can quickly reach massive audiences with a proper launch.

Over the last twenty years, I've examined every possible game that has launched and looked to see if each game fits all three criteria.

A game can have a $1 billion launch day if it meets all three standards. It can generate a $100 million launch with two of the elements. And even if it has just one, it's enough to attract significant attention and an audience.

Of course, these three elements require investment dollars.

And how do games get funded in the current ecosystem?

Today, we have a $200 billion industry driven by large publishers who fund game developers. Historically, the typical

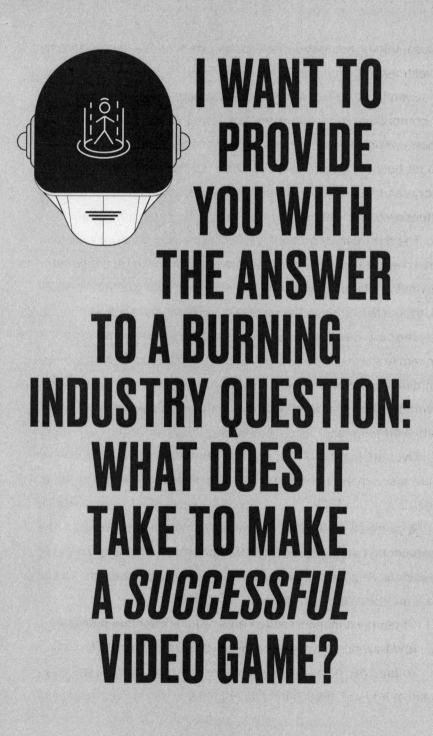

I WANT TO PROVIDE YOU WITH THE ANSWER TO A BURNING INDUSTRY QUESTION: WHAT DOES IT TAKE TO MAKE A *SUCCESSFUL* VIDEO GAME?

agreement—should the development be funded—would see the publisher get 80 percent of the project's revenue while the producer receives just 20 percent. However, the publisher provides most of that capital as an advance, meaning that development costs are ultimately deducted from the producer's revenue stake.

Publishers might want to offer a fifty-fifty deal in a more modern, competitive environment. This structure gave me the idea to compete with the publishers. Rather than see game producers go through a venture capital or publisher approach, Xsolla and other companies like us allow games to go directly to consumers. We also outsource many of the elements that publishers traditionally offer in-house through their agreements, such as servers, payments, public relations, and more.

By outsourcing these components, game producers can focus on developing the best game possible and no longer need to give away 50 percent of their revenue up front. Instead, they can maintain their long-term vision, self-publish the game, and go directly to their audience.

I propose a much smaller revenue share. At Xsolla, I typically seek a revenue share that starts at 10 percent and can range up to 50 percent, depending on the producers' needs, in exchange for working capital. This model allows the video game producer to decide how much funding they require and what tools they need to attract additional investment.

When producing video games, it's important to acknowledge one of the biggest challenges in the sales cycle.

Games typically never ship on time, and many producers want to add additional items as they push toward their release. A revenue share model gives producers flexibility to obtain additional capital to add features, celebrities, or other entities to increase the game's visibility.

I prefer to have control of the 10 percent to 50 percent of the top-line revenue stream instead of equity, the preferred metric of a VC fund. This allows the producers to decide what level of their profit center they want to utilize to continually build their games.

And why will they need the money?

Most games will have a primary release date planned far in advance, like the release of a big box-office event. Highly antic- ipated games tend to experience a large spike in sales for one weekend or series of weeks, and then sales will taper off, with less and less consumption over time.

These games are typically single-player campaigns designed primarily for one or two experiences. The second type of game is more of a service on which multiple iterations will exist. Publishers will produce updates and new worlds on top of the games. But they all need the most complete launch possible to make a real profit.

I'm a big advocate of investing in video game trailers.

Trailers?

Of course, just like a great movie, a video game needs an opportunity to create buzz. Under a trailer revenue share, I prefer to provide capital into the trailer. Upon successful preorders of the game, I can receive that investment back, while the developers are able to generate additional capital for their game development.

It's an opportunity to engage in the three critical needs of every video game:

1. It needs unique mechanics; a good trailer can showcase what makes the game different and the functionality that will excite gamers to experience it.
2. It needs good content; a trailer will capture the story and the essence behind the game.
3. It needs to reach the broadest audience possible; a trailer enables the marketing to create buzz and get people's attention.

Video game trailers are one of my favorite ways to invest in games.

When many developers complete their games, they come to Xsolla to explore ways to develop the best trailer possible.

A great game without great visibility is not a viable product. So, in exchange for a small revenue share, we can help them reach their marketing goals and broaden their launch potential to the widest audience possible. Since we operate like Hollywood, we are the last money in and the first money out for the project.

I'M A BIG ADVOCATE OF INVESTING IN VIDEO GAME TRAILERS. TRAILERS? OF COURSE, JUST LIKE A GREAT MOVIE, A VIDEO GAME NEEDS AN OPPORTUNITY TO CREATE BUZZ.

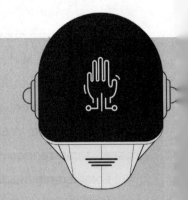

Today, I personally invest in about twelve to twenty deals a year with creative houses to build trailers for video games, and I expect this will be successful and create a snowball effect over time. A good trailer is easily shareable on social media and blogs dedicated to gaming audiences. In addition, it can be picked up by trade magazines or YouTube enthusiasts who will generate buzz and showcase it to millions of potential customers.

I believe this is an incredibly viable business that will produce terrific future results for producers and investors. I aim to scale this concept, as I anticipate that a good team can build a portfolio and game-royalty system to fund upward of one thousand or more independent games a year. It's a simple concept, and it's built on the back of the same strategy that has made my multiple businesses successful: aggregation.

I succeeded by aggregating games and payment options and found this business model very profitable. Many of the most successful businesses are aggregators: Uber aggregates drivers, Airbnb aggregates homes, and Google aggregates information.

In the case of Xsolla, we aggregate the payment systems for games. Now, I want to aggregate every possible source of funding for developers. And we're focused on every possible investor—from retail investors and prospective video game players to institutional players like family offices, qualified investors, and more. Today, we already provide two systems for developers to obtain capital and to maximize their returns.

For example, Xsolla's Funding Club is a matchmaking service for developers, investment firms or groups, and video game publishers. Investors can find the type of projects that interest them and the terms that meet their expectations while giving the developers access to capital and terms depending on the life cycle of their project development. In addition, Xsolla's Game Investment Platform gives investors access to new game details, insight into the monetization model, and insight into the development team.

One of my core beliefs is the importance of treating all participants—both investors and developers—as customers and fighting for them on every front, ranging from payments, chargebacks, managing user acquisitions, taxes in various jurisdictions, compliance, and more. There are many challenges in this business—and I'm obsessed with maximizing opportunities and helping projects reach their full potential. At Xsolla, we want to see more people succeed in their businesses and maximize every dollar possible for their projects so that they can go on to create new successes in the future.

SCAN ME FOR MORE INFO

CHAPTER 12

STORY3: STORYTELLING VIA MICROTRANSACTIONS

Just around the corner from my office in Los Angeles is Fox Plaza.

In 1987, this thirty-four-story tower at 2121 Avenue of the Stars received a temporary nickname. Film producers called it "Nakatomi Plaza" as a set piece for the movie *Die Hard*.

Americans like to debate whether *Die Hard*, released in 1988, is a Christmas movie.

Too many people forget that the film was based on a book called *Nothing Lasts Forever*, an action thriller by the novelist Roderick Thorp.

From a fundamental perspective, the *Die Hard* story is interesting because it combines the two basic archetypal stories of the publishing and film worlds.

The author and literary professor John Gardner once explained the benefit of using one of two approaches when writing a new story: Have a hero go on a journey or have a stranger come to town. In *The Art of Fiction: Notes on Craft for Young Writers*, Gardner advised authors, "Write the opening of a novel using the authorial- omniscient voice, making the authorial omniscience clear by going into the thoughts of one or more characters after establishing the voice. As subject, use either a trip or the arrival of a stranger (some disruption of order—the usual novel beginning)."[117]

While everyone is focused on the journey of *Die Hard*'s John McClane, portrayed by Bruce Willis, the arrival of the stranger Hans Gruber (portrayed by Alan Rickman) in Los Angeles sets the movie's tone. It moves the story (and the chaos) forward.

As you can tell, I love stories.

In fiction, I admire authors who develop ideas for the page or screen, start with a character, give the character motivation, and take them on a journey. Or, the stranger arrives in town, and the rest of the characters must adjust to the changes thrust on them.

Examples of the hero's journey include *Star Wars*, the *Hunger Games* trilogy, *Harry Potter*, *Spiderman*, *Lord of the Rings*, the *Matrix* series, *Big Fish*, the *Wizard of Oz*, and even *Harold & Kumar Go to White Castle*.

Examples of when the stranger arrives include *Footloose*, *Demolition Man*, the *Lethal Weapon* franchise, *Meet Joe Black*, the *Legend of Bagger Vance*, and weather disaster movies.

On the nonfiction side, I appreciate journalists and documentarians.

Those practices remain under intense global scrutiny, and speaking truth to power is difficult. Whether someone is writing about the economy or social issues, it is incredibly challenging. The job requires extraordinary patience, time management, and creativity.

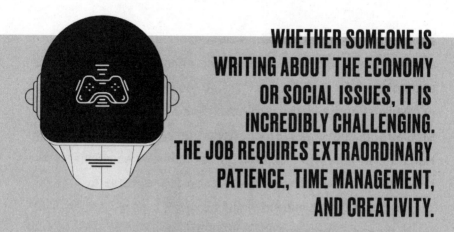

WHETHER SOMEONE IS WRITING ABOUT THE ECONOMY OR SOCIAL ISSUES, IT IS INCREDIBLY CHALLENGING. THE JOB REQUIRES EXTRAORDINARY PATIENCE, TIME MANAGEMENT, AND CREATIVITY.

Over the last two decades, news publishing has changed dramatically. Newspapers and magazines have scaled back to focus heavily on digital operations. Advertising has dried up in traditional media outlets, with large outlets scaling back their newsroom desks.

The same trend has picked up in print journals that feature short-story writing. At the same time, book publishers drift further toward digital models to reduce costs and prioritize best sellers and stories that attract Hollywood interest.

From the outside looking in, this may be one of the most challenging periods in history to be a write—and to do so with financial success. If you're a writer, you're familiar with the challenges I will outline. But, once we recognize the problems of most writers, we can build solutions that reward writers and publishers for their creativity.

In addition, we can create a user experience that builds direct audiences for writers and cuts out the middleman and centralized platforms like the Web 2.0 producers of today.

THE CHALLENGE OF CONSOLIDATION

The shift toward digital and online media has starved most companies of advertising dollars and fueled incredible consolidation of publishing houses over the last two decades.

This transition has left many writers with challenges, including a lack of full-time work, unpredictable income streams, and questions about the industry's future. This isn't limited to just the written word. It extends to publishing roles of all stripes: Line editors, graphic designers, film editors, and more.

In today's media environment, creative types must spend countless hours networking, building portfolios, marketing content, writing query letters, and locating new clients. Once they secure work, they must then manage deadline expectations, walk the fine line between the client's needs and their creative views, and handle revisions to any work.

Just consider the process of creating new editorial work for a fiction or nonfiction publisher of a simple 800-word article or 1,500-word short story.

The writers must research publishers that might consider their work. This will require drafting a cover letter that speaks directly to the publication's previous coverage of similar topics or stories (which requires significant time reading other work).

Since these articles are typically unsolicited, they must locate publishers that will accept such a query. In addition, the writer must meet all guidelines around word count, deadlines, and formats.

The article or short story must be immaculate, carefully edited, and written to comply with the publisher's style. It should have no typos, feature active tense for nearly all sentences, and contain zero grammatical mistakes.

The author will soon submit the letter and article. And then, the waiting game begins. Responses could take weeks, depending on the volume of submissions handled by the publisher. A news story, opinion piece, or original concept centered on a recent headline could quickly grow stale in just a few days. After all that work, the success rate might be low, or the author might need to settle for much lower pay than the initial target price.

This is a very time-consuming industry and one that can over-whelm writers and editors quickly. It can also fail to justify the time spent should the financial payoff not align.

The consumer journey can be just as challenging.

For years, readers turned to trusted media brands for their news.

Magazines like *Newsweek* and *Time* dominated the circulation wars of the 1980s and 1990s. Television news centered on four channels in the early 1990s.

Now, so many news outlets exist that knowing where to turn is difficult. In addition, most media outlets have their own bias, their ideological or political tilt. The massive shift toward digital media has dried up circulations and placed a greater focus on catering directly to a core audience based on demographics. As a result, nearly every media outlet online today is starving for revenue.

Sign onto the websites of the *New York Times* or the *Washington Post*; you might receive two free articles each month as an unpaid reader.

Try to read a third article, and the site will prompt you to make a subscription payment. Again, these sites are not alone. Nearly every major media outlet has shifted toward a paid online model over the last few years.

Want a deeper analysis of your favorite sports team on ESPN? The ESPN Plus subscription will cost $120 per year.

Want to read more about finance and the stock market on Bloomberg? With a monthly subscription, it will cost $360 per year.

There was a time that you could buy a copy of the *Wall Street Journal* for $2.00 at the newsstand. Unfortunately, it'll cost you over $100 annually if you want a digital subscription (no physical paper included). The news site will also pummel your browser with advertisements and may swarm your computer with push notification messages.

The news is not a public service. It's a business model.

A better model is about to emerge in the future.

And blockchain and microtransactions can serve as a driver of what is now possible.

MICROTRANSACTIONS AND THE STORY3 POTENTIAL

Publishers, storytellers, journalists, and writers of all stripes could soon earn real compensation for their work through a project I'm launching called *Story3*.

Through traditional online publishing, readers can check out a few introductory paragraphs to stories and decide if they like what they read. If they do, readers can make a micropayment of five to ten cents to keep reading.

What are micropayments? Let's review them with a little more depth.

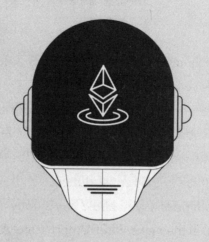

THE NEWS IS NOT A PUBLIC SERVICE. IT IS A BUSINESS MODEL.

Micropayments are a very successful part of the video game financial model.

In traditional video games, publishers sell virtual items or in-game currencies in exchange for dollars and other money. Typically, buyers complete these transactions in an online store within the game's platform. Over time, these transactions will be tracked on the blockchain to confirm the purchases and ensure the authenticity of all digital items.

Once someone purchases an item, it is added to a digital wallet or inventory. These microtransactions have a wide range of possibilities. Some players will buy skins and clothing for their avatars. Others might pay for upgrades to weapons, player health, or other experience boosts. Some players might even pay for tools to bypass a level or unlock an achievement. The latter two elements interest me: the chance to move forward in the story, like how someone moves forward through a video game with a transaction.

In publishing, microtransactions can provide similar positive experiences for customers.

Media outlets could use microtransactions to monetize their content. Instead of relying on Pay-Per-Click (PPC) advertising models or email marketing of their customer lists, microtransactions could allow users to pay for premium content.

Readers could pay a small amount for in-depth interviews, exclusive videos, or behind-the-scenes looks at stories. In addition, these transactions can help a publisher identify their most engaged readers and viewers.

This not only helps a publisher understand who will pay for content but also establishes a loyalty program for this audience and creates exclusive opportunities for this readership. As I've noted, all businesses need to build a more loyal following among the 20 percent of customers who produce 80 percent of the revenue.

The only way to properly understand those customers is to engage them, understand their preferences, explore their purchasing behaviors, and adapt a content strategy moving forward. I'm not convinced that a straight microtransaction model specifically for traditional media outlets will benefit storytellers and writers within the publishing ecosystem.

I want the storytellers, the writers, and the content producers to benefit the most.

Here's the thing: when it comes to publishing, no shortage of online pages exists.

This isn't like operating a newspaper in 1980. There isn't a finite amount of space for print today. We're not wasting paper by publishing as many stories as possible online.

All that we have done is publish a story to a new webpage in just a few clicks. And, rather than have a publisher capitalize on it and pay the writer for a onetime report, this article or story can exist online forever and serve as a revenue source into perpetuity for the writer.

The entire premise—again—relies on offering writers a chance to move away from the traditional "work-for-hire" model. For example, would a writer prefer to receive a payment of $100 one time for an article of seven hundred words, or would they prefer to receive five cents for every reader for the next twenty years? This would require two thousand readers to pay five cents to break even.

But if ten thousand readers enjoy an article or story, this quickly translates into $500—or five times the money.

In addition, the content belongs to the writer, which is critical in the future. For example, consider a situation where a writer drafts a long story about an important social issue. Perhaps it's a journalism project that uncovers a significant political mishap that impacts thousands of citizens. Imagine that this story goes viral, generating tens of thousands of views.

That work should belong to the author, not the media outlet that will enjoy the clicks and views. Now, imagine that a major Hollywood studio wants to buy the rights to this story.

In the traditional film world, the Hollywood game would require the author to share a significant portion of the story rights with the media outlet.

I don't see common sense any more in that traditional business model.

Authors should have complete control of their work and the rights to the story, especially freelance writers who have no full-time relationship with the outlet. Unfortunately, however, this happens quite often.

The same goes for book authors who sell the rights to their novels or nonfiction stories to Hollywood. Again, the publishing house receives a large chunk of this revenue, even if the author did all the work, created all the characters, conducted all the research, and interviewed all the subjects. This business model doesn't make sense to me, given the current opportunities and technologies that make it easier than ever for writers to build their brands.

> **AUTHORS SHOULD HAVE COMPLETE CONTROL OF THEIR WORK AND THE RIGHTS TO THE STORY, ESPECIALLY FREELANCE WRITERS WHO HAVE NO FULL-TIME RELATIONSHIP WITH THE OUTLET. UNFORTUNATELY, HOWEVER, THIS HAPPENS QUITE OFTEN.**

THE POWER OF DECENTRALIZING CONTENT DELIVERY AND CREATION

The last decade has fueled an incredible rise in media platforms that allow for the broad production and dissemination of stories. The Netflix model has taken box office films from the theaters and placed them directly into consumers' homes. Amazon's Kindle has enabled the widespread dissemination of digital books, cutting down on trips to Barnes and Noble and reducing the amount of paper required. The media platforms and aggregators have fueled the shift from the printed word to the digital word.

With the shift to Web 3.0 and the more decentralized nature of technology moving forward, I predict a major change in content delivery and content creation. As we move away from centralized platforms to decentralized platforms, the shift will center more on the development of stories instead of where they are published. In addition, the shift will tilt more favorably on the compensation model that rewards the storyteller and less on the middleman platform that has extracted most of the revenue from the content producers.

I have started to create Story3, a platform that empowers writers to post brief introductions to stories. People can read those introductory paragraphs without ads and with no contractual commitment. Then, if they enjoy the story, they can have options for reading it.

Readers can read half of the page of the story and proceed with nanotransactions that allow them to decide how much more they would like to read. For example, authors can create an introduction to the story. They can then present options for the users that will include a free version of the story, an upgraded payment of the story that will consist of more detail, or a complete version of the story that might include different endings, quotes, plot twists, or depth to the story that would be more enhanced than the previous versions.

This model will not include advertising. It will not involve subscriptions. Instead, it will entirely live off the concept of micro-transactions. If consumers don't like a story, they can turn to the next story.

But more importantly, this can provide an ecosystem of content creation and collaboration. Story3 can evolve into a system that rewards original authors for their contributions and into more complex storylines that can translate into film, comics, or other artwork that complements creative design and development.

For example, picture this. A writer in California can start writing a story with different variations. There could be a free short story, a second post with more detail, and a third, more complete story that starts to incorporate more creative input from other content producers. A content creator in Sao Paulo, Brazil, might create the spoken version of the story in Portuguese. An artist in Nigeria may create visual content that complements the story. A graphic designer in Dallas might collaborate with a musician in the United Kingdom to provide additional artwork or visual shorts that will become part of the paid version of the story.

The possibilities are endless for storytelling and compensation. Over time, this system can involve artificial intelligence to translate languages, improve grammar, and address spelling. This also allows for collaborations among individuals who create in different media and contribute to the story's evolution. These contributions can come from writing, music, art, AI, or other media. I hope that great stories can evolve much like the video games forged to become $500 million businesses through the collaboration of twenty people.

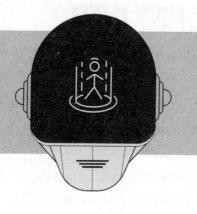

THE POSSIBILITIES ARE ENDLESS FOR STORYTELLING AND COMPENSATION.

Furthermore, the contributions of each can be measured across the blockchain, and contributors can receive direct compensation. The people who create the story will receive payment through microtransactions. The people who acquire the audience and deliver them to the site can receive compensation through social media channels. And the affiliate who takes part in the process will receive compensation.

The future of blockchain is limitless, and the platforms that have dominated content distribution over the last decade will start to lose their power. Moving forward, decentralized platforms that enhance storytelling and incentivize the medium's power will become the dominant revenue model. I hope new partners join Story3 for the incredible ride ahead.

SCAN ME FOR MORE INFO

CHAPTER 13

I LOVE LA—AND SO DOES THE METAVERSE

Los Angeles has a semi-arid, Mediterranean-like climate.

It rarely rains in the summer. To the southeast and direct north, long stretches of drought hit the region. But there's something hypnotic about the rain when it comes to LA

The sky quickly becomes overcast. The air suddenly cools and feels damp.

As the rain begins, a soft pattering follows across the sidewalks and roofs. It sounds at first like children running after a ball. Then the rain grows louder and faster—a burst of intensity.

The pace can be frantic. It's the perfect metaphor for how an idea starts to run wild in a storyteller's mind. The way that a single snowflake can trigger an avalanche. It's how I imagine a writer or artist runs wild with an idea, building on its intensity, getting every detail possible onto paper or onto a canvas. Until it finally peters out.

I love Los Angeles. Every small detail.

It's one of the most diverse cities on the planet, with a wide range of cultural perspectives and unlimited creative expression.

People flock here from all around the world to collaborate and pursue their passions.

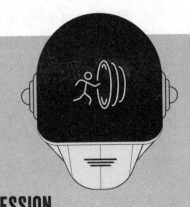

I LOVE LOS ANGELES. EVERY SMALL DETAIL. IT'S ONE OF THE MOST DIVERSE CITIES ON THE PLANET, WITH A WIDE RANGE OF CULTURAL PERSPECTIVES AND UNLIMITED CREATIVE EXPRESSION.

Geographically, I can't think of a better place for a creative mind.

Within an hour, you can drive from downtown LA to Santa Monica Beach or Huntington Beach, dip your toes in the surf, and look out onto the vast Pacific Ocean.

In two hours, you can reach the desert park of Joshua Tree. There you can hike and rock climb, while surrounding yourself with cacti and starlit skies.

To the north, you can visit the San Bernardino Mountains, hike long trails through the thick forest of pine trees, and take in the gorgeous views.

Also, a half dozen winter ski resorts are within a two-hour drive.

If nature isn't your thing, the drive up the Pacific Coast Highway (PCH) from Los Angeles to Malibu is one of the most incredible stretches of road on the planet. The warm sun shines brightly over the Pacific, and along the way you'll see countless surfers paddling against the tide and riding massive waves.

For those who prefer to stay downtown, the city has one of the most vibrant cultures in North America—with museums, theaters, and music venues stretched across its landscape. Local and international artists connect and perform their shows and exhibits across a vast infrastructure.

This is the home of modern film and television, and it has always offered similar foundations for musicians, production studios, and other performance artists. Here, the vibrance shows in every element of the creative ecosystem. Waiters and baristas end their shifts and head to television and film auditions.

Some nights, you may notice a valet editing a script they've written.

People from all walks of life are pursuing their creative dreams here.

As we migrate from today's economy to the Metaverse, I can't think of another place that could quickly transition into the international capital of this technological movement.

As I'll explain, I believe the Metaverse infrastructure of Los Angeles will ultimately surpass the older model of tech companies in Silicon Valley.

Let's unpack the opportunity for the City of Angels.

A CITY OF LIMITLESS POTENTIAL

I moved to Los Angeles in 2010 because of the life I wanted to lead.

As I mentioned in chapter 2, growing up in Russia, I watched Hollywood movies and viewed them as a window to a better world.

And when you come from a place of secrecy and move to an area rife with storytelling and possibilities, it feels like you're living in a movie with a happy ending.

Los Angeles's influence over the power of narrative and storytelling is unlike anywhere else in the world.

There isn't even a close second-place city on a scale of Los Angeles' magnitude. Every day, I'm reminded—anywhere I go—that so many parts of this city have acted as tools to help great content producers tell entertaining stories.

Near my office sits the Sherman Oaks Galleria, which served as a set location for the films *Terminator 2* and *Commando* in the 1980s. Sometimes, I can't believe I'm walking the same streets as the superheroes portrayed by Arnold Schwarzenegger.

In Century City there's the "Nakatomi Plaza," a large office building that opened in 1987. The following year, it was the fictional headquarters of the Nakatomi Corporation, a made-up company in the hit movie *Die Hard*. Those who live in City of Angels know the real name of this place is Fox Plaza. Fans of the Bruce Willis movie franchise still visit regularly, take pictures of the famous building, and call it by its movie name.

Then, there are the landmarks that remind me of the possibilities in Hollywood. For example, the Beverly Hills Hotel is a five-star hotel off West Sunset Boulevard. Today, a room might cost more than $2,000 per night.

In the 1960s, a young actor named Robert Evans checked into the hotel. He initially worked as an actor and model in Los Angeles, but Evans also had an eye for talent and turned his attention to film production. He produced several acclaimed movies that decade, including *Rosemary's Baby* and *Love Story*.

By 1966, the great film studio Paramount Pictures was facing financial challenges. It had undergone dramatic changes to its executive team. Recognizing Evans's talent, Paramount nominated him to become the head of production at the company.

Evans was a modern businessman on top of being a great storyteller. He would go on to modernize Paramount Pictures, focus on making competitive films at the box office, and carry Hollywood through a difficult transition. During Evans's tenure, Paramount dominated for roughly fifteen years, releasing two of the greatest films of all time—*The Godfather* and *Chinatown*. Both films earned eleven Oscar nominations each, and *The Godfather* won the Academy Award for Best Picture.

When I look at Los Angeles, I see the glamour, and I see the grit.

These two things are not mutually exclusive. To be a storyteller is a daily grind—writing, acting, scene-building, and producing. So many people fail one day, get up the next day, and chase the same dream to pursue their calling. It's incredibly inspiring.

SO MANY PEOPLE FAIL ONE DAY, GET UP THE NEXT DAY, AND CHASE THE SAME DREAM TO PURSUE THEIR CALLING.

I'll also drive around the Avenue of the Stars in Century City or past the Hollywood Walk of Fame. Here, Hollywood legends are honored with a star on the walkway with their name (and typically their handprints) to memorialize and lionize their contributions to film production. I can't help but notice how many people are working toward that goal.

Occasionally, I'll see a fast muscle car roaring up Hollywood Boulevard or Sunset Boulevard and instantly think about the rise and prominence of super-agent Michael Ovitz, who cofounded the powerful Creative Artists Agency (CAA).

Ovitz's love for luxury cars is well known.

In his prime, he reportedly owned five different Jaguars, which he drove on different days of the week. His red, yellow, blue, green, or black Jaguar would match the color of his clothing for the day. This story became so widely known that it helped establish Ovitz's reputation and brand as a powerful creative agent.

In many ways, his love of the Jaguar brand combined with his creative expression in the physical world is a perfect example of how I see people engaging with luxury brands in the Metaverse to express their personalities and how they want to be seen.

Hollywood has the talent. It has the infrastructure. It has countless stories. Anyone can shoot a timeless film anywhere within a hundred miles of this city and create instant success, as I've witnessed in the video game industry. And it's my goal to give people the tools they need to bring their stories and characters to life.

Los Angeles should be the capital of the Metaverse transition for our world.

As I've mentioned in previous chapters, when it comes to the Metaverse, most of the technology has already been developed. And new layers will emerge in the years and decades ahead. What the Metaverse needs—its lifeblood—will be great storytellers.

WHY LA AND THE METAVERSE MAKE SENSE

Storytelling is far more important than servers, semiconductors, or computers. To help you better understand the potential impact of the Metaverse, I want to break this conversation down into two primary streams of expectations:

1. The macroeconomic and social factors
2. The dramatic impact on storytelling itself

I'll start with the big picture of why the television and film ecosystem of Los Angeles will make a successful transition into the Metaverse.

First, let's remember that movies are brands themselves.

For example, *Star Wars* goes well beyond the visual narrative presented on the big screen. There is now a massive *Star Wars* theme park within the Disney World experience.

In previous chapters, I discussed how a company like Adidas might make interactive experiences for soccer fans. Well, Hollywood will take this expectation to the next level.

The *Star Wars* franchise could create Metasites that provide next-generation experiences, allowing fans to explore the imaginary worlds of the franchise's films and television series. For example, fans could visit the film's famous Mos Eisley cantina and determine if Han shot first.

The Metaverse will allow any film franchise—big budget or independent—to offer similar experiences for fans to meet characters, go on adventures, or explore the history and richness of the story.

I've mentioned *The Godfather*, which is still recognized as one of the greatest films of all time. Imagine the opportunity for fans to sit virtually across the desk with Vito Corleone on the day of his daughter's wedding. As I'll explain, these small experiences will be central to expanding on the characters' universe, enhancing the potential longevity of the franchise and creating new revenue opportunities.

Adoption of these Metaverse offerings can instantly open new revenue streams for film franchises even decades after they were blockbuster hits. For example, franchises can sell virtual items like NFTs, clothing, and exclusive experiences and events. Such occasions might include access to behind-the-scenes footage or exclusive opportunities for fans to meet the actors and producers. More than anything, they represent a chance to cater directly to the most loyal fans who are willing to spend the money.

Second, there's an opportunity that means so much to me personally.

The Metaverse will allow many film and television franchises to live forever, expanding their reach beyond the traditional storylines and into the engaging and immersive new world of the Metaverse. What does this mean? In a moment, I'll explain how the Metaverse will enable creative producers to unlock films that have never seen the light of day.

But in this case, I'm talking about the possibility of extending the films' storylines and their characters. Movie franchises will have the potential to create new and interactive content. Think about the opportunity for fans to explore characters' backstories.

What would it be like to interact with Forrest Gump on his Alabama farm and see the famous tree where Forrest and Jenny used to chat?

What does it mean for a fan of the Avengers to choose their own superpowers and go on adventures with the characters?

What possibilities exist when you give the storyteller more than a couple of hours to tell a story about the characters and the world in which they operate?

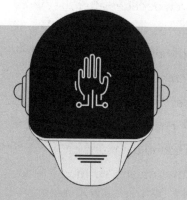

WHAT POSSIBILITIES EXIST WHEN YOU GIVE THE STORYTELLER MORE THAN A COUPLE OF HOURS TO TELL A STORY ABOUT THE CHARACTERS AND THE WORLD IN WHICH THEY OPERATE?

What would it feel like to sit on the lowest deck of the *Titanic* with Leonardo DiCaprio's character and understand his view as a young man from a small Wisconsin town compared to the wealthier, big-city characters up on the main deck?

What could you learn about that character?

How would it alter your understanding of that period, of class and culture, and of the disaster in the mid-Atlantic in April 1912?

There is a limitless opportunity for creators and developers to bring all the backstory and motivations of characters to life in the Metaverse—and establish living memorials for these characters that go far beyond what traditional film can convey.

But it's not just the films in existence today.

It's also about the movies that remain tucked away in the basement of traditional film studios.

When I think about all the great movies I've seen in my lifetime, I realize how many I *haven't* seen.

Pick any studio you want in Los Angeles, and you'll quickly learn they are sitting on a gold mine of content. For every movie that a studio makes, there are hundreds of scripts that it never produced, including film franchises that never saw the chance to extend beyond one film.

There could be thousands of stories that have never been revealed to the world, dating back decades. An untold number of characters are locked in time capsules, and the Metaverse can finally reveal them to the world.

Through the Metaverse, it would be relatively inexpensive to put these scripts out into the world, license them, and allow Metaverse producers to develop them. Furthermore, any film-maker looking for a budget will have the opportunity to fund and monetize their films through revenue shares and unique agreements that help build the universe of their movies.

THE NEW GOLDEN AGE

Finally, I want to explain the three key things that can make this future possible and profitable for Hollywood producers through Metasites:

1. The characters
2. The digital items
3. The environment

An incredible amount of money and potential exists with these three elements.

Let's start with the characters.

In the future, most people will likely not be able to tell the difference between a video of a real person speaking and a video of artificial intelligence (AI). Of course, some people are worried about this—but in this world of Hollywood, I think it offers limitless potential.

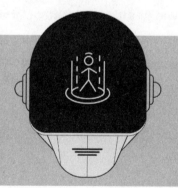

IN THE FUTURE, THE OPPORTUNITY TO REENGAGE WITH THE AUDIENCE WILL BE UNLIKE ANYTHING EVER WITNESSED.

Artificial intelligence advancements will allow us to monetize the digital likeness of past characters and actors. And anyone who owns and operates the estate of Hollywood's greatest actors will quickly recognize the importance of monetizing those legacies.

In the future, the opportunity to reengage with the audience will be unlike anything ever witnessed. One of the greatest inventions in history was Johannes Gutenberg's printing press in 1436, which made it possible to mass-produce books and disseminate them worldwide. This fueled the proliferation of the Bible around the globe and made the works of William Shakespeare available on every continent by the mid-seventeenth century.

Artificial intelligence will outpace the printing press in every way—as it continually learns and grows. In fact, it's been said that AI's power and speed double every six months.[118]

So, in twelve months, AI will be four times more powerful than it is today.

In four years, AI will be 256 times more powerful than it is today. With such advancements comes the opportunity to accelerate the potential of this technology.

I propose straightforward projects today that bring characters of past films and television to life. Whether it's in a chatbot or a digital experience, fans will be able to have real conversations with characters. Those conversations will require today's storytellers to see how these characters would react.

How do they talk?

What do they think?

How do they feel?

What questions would they avoid?

What would make them blush?

These questions are vital to developing characters in the Metaverse and to creating incredible storytelling opportunities that will offer lasting experiences for decades.

As we create these characters, there is ample opportunity to develop the environments in which they exist. For example, with Metasites, consider the possibility of where these characters would live. Storytellers can help build these environments and provide input into even the most subtle details of a character's background.

Suppose a fan visits a Metasite that takes them into the home of a famous character. In that case, every detail is critical—and every element might warrant a response in a conversation.

Imagine that you step into the university office of Professor Henry "Indiana" Jones from the films *Raiders of the Lost Ark* and *Indiana Jones and the Last Crusade*. A conversation between the two of you might occur at a crowded desk from the 1930s. It might be covered with papers and artifacts. On the shelf in the background, there might be parts of a treasure he uncovered somewhere in the Middle East. Professor Jones will likely have an answer if you ask about that tiny detail. Better yet, as the Metaverse unfolds, he might even be able to take you on an adventure.

And this is just one example of one character in one film franchise.

The potential for storytelling is limitless.

It could be a universe for Han Solo, Terminator, James Bond, Ellen Ripley, Captain Jack Sparrow, Bruce Wayne, John McClane, Tyler Durden, Vito Corleone, Marty McFly, or Doc Brown.

The AI will enable storytellers to expand on all of them—*and* characters who don't yet exist today. These characters can travel across environments, interact with each other, and create experiences for fans across the Metaverse.

But it doesn't just have to be around fiction.

The Metaverse can help documentarians provide deeper detail and insight into their investigations and stories.

In the world of true crime, the Metaverse can give producers and directors a chance to showcase real-life mysteries and allow viewers to investigate murders. Imagine a world in which you can tag along with a detective to look for clues, add items to their digital wallet, and put together a puzzle from the past.

This brings us to the monetization element that emerges in digital items.

In the world of Metasites, storytellers can monetize items that can expand on the story. Creators can import their most popular characters and stories into the Metaverse and share in the revenues that are generated. There will be opportunities to directly engage the most loyal fans and invite them with special NFTs to unique, custom experiences. Digital items can develop the marketing potential and incentivize users to dig deeper into the worlds created by storytellers.

Viewers who want the most immersive experience of the characters and environment will gladly spend money to dive deeper into the world of storytelling. They will come to know characters in the Metaverse the same way avid readers view great authors as friends.

AI will produce massive levels of written, spoken, and visual content. The challenge and the opportunity are to give people a real, immersive experience that draws them back repeatedly.

The Metaverse can drag users away from fifteen-second TikTok videos and constant scrolling of Twitter and social media sites. In contrast to these platforms, the Metaverse is a limitless playground for users to immerse themselves in something more profound, interactive, and breathtaking.

Looking forward, creative storytellers will shape the Metaverse and give the world a deeper understanding of their characters and process.

For all Los Angeles writers, content producers, directors, and individuals who want to tell a story, I invite you to take part in this movement. For others outside of the Los Angeles area who share the same storytelling ambitions, I encourage you to get in touch as well.

I will work with you. I will produce with you. I will help you develop the tools to bring these Metasites to life in ways that you are just starting to imagine.

The Metaverse will create the new Golden Age of Hollywood.

THE METAVERSE WILL CREATE THE NEW GOLDEN AGE OF HOLLYWOOD.

All you have to do is take the first step.

CHAPTER 14

FINAL THOUGHTS: SEIZING THE OPPORTUNITIES OF THE METAVERSE

We've discussed the opportunities for storytellers, content producers, creative minds, and entrepreneurs in the Metaverse. This new world will be life-changing.

I've also shared my personal experiences.

I've discussed my humble beginnings in Russia and how video games changed my life. We explored my move to the United States and how it transformed my understanding of what remains possible thanks to technology, video games, and entrepreneurialism.

I witnessed the success many entrepreneurs, venture capitalists, and consumers enjoyed with the dawn of the internet and the rise of digital technologies.

Still, I have never seen an opportunity like the Metaverse.

While the internet served as the great equalizer for me over the last twenty years, the Metaverse will likely serve as an even greater force for economic and social good in the world. I am eager to witness how the Metaverse will change how we socialize, fundraise for charities, educate people of all ages, and create sustainable brands.

WHILE THE INTERNET SERVED AS THE GREAT EQUALIZER FOR ME OVER THE LAST TWENTY YEARS, THE METAVERSE WILL LIKELY SERVE AS AN EVEN GREATER FORCE FOR ECONOMIC AND SOCIAL GOOD IN THE WORLD.

I foresee an incredible opportunity to turn the next iteration of the internet into a tremendous source of good for eight billion people. In addition to these social goals, the Metaverse should center on people earning more money and exploring their passions.

And the financial opportunity is simply unmatched.

In the decade ahead, as I've mentioned, the Metaverse could provide upward of $10 trillion to $30 trillion in economic opportunity worldwide, according to estimates by Citigroup and Epyllion CEO Matthew Ball.[119]

Anyone with an idea, a brand, a story, and a vision can now apply them to the Metaverse and start building toward a much brighter future.

My vision of the Metaverse doesn't start or stop with one entrepreneur like Meta Platforms CEO Mark Zuckerberg. It's not centralized. Big Silicon Valley companies will not dominate it. It doesn't operate through one type of technology like VR headsets.

The Metaverse is the extension of multiple digital worlds and cutting-edge technologies. It will build on the latest generation of video game technologies and virtual worlds. It will allow anyone to immerse themselves and experience a growing, global community that forever changes how we work, play, shop, explore, and engage brands. This isn't one person's ecosystem to dominate and control.

It will infinitely differ from the internet and the world we know today.

As I've explained, interoperability will allow users to explore multiple worlds and take their digital items with them. The blockchain will enhance the security of transactions, increase transparency among parties, protect digital identities, and verify ownership of scarce things like NFTs, real estate, and more. In addition, the decentralized nature of the Metaverse will ensure that no one company or group of companies controls it. The power will be shared among the creators and cocreators crafting the assets across the Metaverse.

We can say goodbye to the centralized internet control of search giants like Google, software titans like Microsoft, entertainment platforms like Spotify and Apple Music, or video game corporations like Activision Blizzard or EA Sports.

The Metaverse will allow individuals to explore virtual and physical worlds in a way that transcends their imaginations. Technologies like the digital cave will offer users the feeling of instant transportation to historical events, museums, live concerts, sports games, and places beyond the reach of our galaxy.

The Metaverse will allow us to visit the future. We can explore what technology and society may evolve toward in the coming centuries or touch down on the terra of Mars and anywhere else that once seemed out of reach.

The Metaverse is an incredible opportunity for musicians and artists to engage their top fans. The 80/20 revenue model—which suggests that 20 percent of a core audience pays 80 percent of a company's revenue—will be central to the success of brands and businesses. The Metaverse will allow artists to feature live virtual events, reward their most loyal fans, and host parties and experiences—all without anyone ever leaving their homes.

The Metaverse will also alter the ways that people socialize.

In the post-COVID era, more people stay home, and travel and hospitality costs are rising. The Metaverse will allow users to connect with other like-minded individuals worldwide. They'll be able to showcase their favorite brands and interact with others who share similar stories, values, and dreams.

Perhaps users will play games together; people will work from home in a different way. The bottom line is that this technology will transcend our imaginations and unleash a powerful new tool that unites people and communities anytime, anywhere.

We're just getting started with the possibilities.

The Metaverse can provide a limitless horizon for people to build and create within virtual worlds. We will see incredible efforts by people to design entire digital cities and ecosystems. This is already underway in various projects like *Minecraft* and *Decentraland*. In addition, users will find real incentives to create

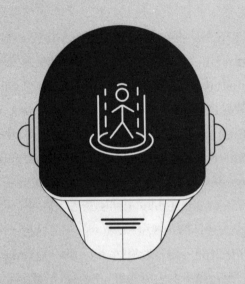

THE METAVERSE CAN PROVIDE A LIMITLESS HORIZON FOR PEOPLE TO BUILD AND CREATE WITHIN VIRTUAL WORLDS.

their avatars, explore new products, shop in a revolutionary manner, and communicate with friends at all hours.

Brands are already creating their digital footprint across the Metaverse. Large companies, from Nike to Adidas, and Crate & Barrel to Gucci, recognize that consumers will migrate to this technology as it becomes more convenient, affordable, and immersive.

However, this new gold rush is only getting started. Hollywood has an incredible opportunity to extend franchise life cycles. Artificial intelligence will breathe new life into characters and their respective worlds. There is limitless potential for creative minds.

Meanwhile, I expect that technology will continue to become a commodity. Over the last few decades, increasing costs have made it difficult for individuals to start businesses and compete against large Silicon Valley giants. As technology advances and prices decline, it will be possible for anyone to create their versions of the companies that dominate today's media environment.

Do you want to have your own Netflix channel dedicated to television and AI-driven films? That will be possible. The cost of making movies will likely decline precipitously as AI advances and technology improves production quality.

This will place an even greater focus on the need for individuals who can tell stories and embrace the decentralized power of the Metaverse.

Of course, with decentralization comes several challenges that this industry must address in the future. I am eager to participate in the necessary discussions around the evolution of the Metaverse and issues around ethics, for example.

As we migrate toward a decentralized, interoperable world, the Metaverse will—like any society—require laws, regulations, and ethics codes.

A simple principle of ethics that transfers across the Metaverse will evolve, helping users understand acceptable versus unacceptable behavior. These rules must center on how individuals treat each other publicly and explore broader issues around intellectual property, data privacy, and human rights.

Technology and commerce move much faster than the regulatory system.

There will be hiccups along the way with business standards, consumer protections, and other regulatory oversight. Again, data privacy, consumer privacy, and Metaverse contract law matters will require deeper regulatory conversations.

However, I am confident that blockchain technology can alleviate several problems around privacy, contract enforcement, data protection, and intellectual property, as I explained in previous chapters.

Over time, plenty of books and conferences will center on these topics. Historically, legal experts, business leaders, philosophers, and ethical advocates have dramatically emerged with new technologies and ecosystems. A robust effort to educate and empower users will continue to gain steam. That will take time, and the regulatory and educational framework will proliferate as the Metaverse accelerates into our day-to-day lives.

This is why you should start thinking about your goals in the Metaverse.

How can you make money?

How can you contribute to its growth?

How can you start your journey right away and grow alongside it?

If you're serious about building a brand, telling your story, besting your competition, and taking part in a digital revolution with more power than the internet or mobile phones, then the time to get started in the Metaverse is now.

Everyone has a story.

And building a Metasite is your opportunity to explore the possibilities of next-generation storytelling.

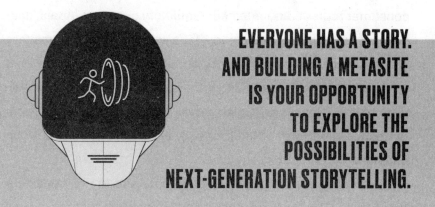

EVERYONE HAS A STORY. AND BUILDING A METASITE IS YOUR OPPORTUNITY TO EXPLORE THE POSSIBILITIES OF NEXT-GENERATION STORYTELLING.

The Metaverse is just a few years away from wide-scale adoption. The competition will increase as it grows more popular and more companies expand their presence.

Now is the time to get ahead of more prominent brands and rival entrepreneurs. If you start building now—especially a Metasite—you will own this property and establish your reputation as a pioneer or early prospector in the Metaverse.

People will talk about how expensive digital real estate and cryptocurrencies are in 2034. Imagine saying how easy it was to start ten years prior.

It will be like saying you bought real estate in Manhattan in the 1970s, bought Bitcoin in 2011 for under $500, or bought a website URL worth hundreds of thousands of dollars for under $10 a decade prior.

Building in the Metaverse will allow users to extend their brand awareness immediately. Metasites will enable businesses to showcase products and services, engage with their top followers and customers, and create immersive experiences that bring people back again and again. By embracing the power of blockchain, you can create customized NFTs and other digital items that bring users closer to your brand.

Adding a Metaverse strategy naturally creates a new revenue stream for any business. Metasites will provide users a unique way to blend the physical and digital worlds as well as allow companies to cross-promote products and services in the two forms.

Metasites will also provide storytellers and brand managers the opportunity to create and innovate in ways that transcend traditional sales and marketing strategies. Your Metasite might allow users to hang out and socialize, get to know you better, and help develop a loyal following as you ramp up your business.

But the most critical question for today is, Why should I be in the Metaverse now?

You want to future-proof your brand immediately.

You want to be ahead of the curve as the Metaverse becomes a critical part of our daily lives in the years and decades ahead.

If you're a consumer, you'll want to participate in the revolution early. You'll want to race ahead of the crowd, build relationships with brands, experience the rewards of interacting with companies in the Metaverse, and build your presence while it's still relatively inexpensive compared to a decade from now.

Remember, economics operates on the simple laws of supply and demand. Right now, supply is increasing, and the market is still lagging. The opportunity to be one of the first to own NFTs, digital goods and items, and much more in the Metaverse is like buying beach property and watching a massive community build around you over the years that follow.

At Xsolla, we've consistently been ahead of the curve and want to help provide users and companies with the tools they need to make this a successful transition. My company accelerated these tools through the video gaming industry for over two decades. In addition, Xsolla has used tools to boost revenue and engage our top buyers.

We plan to do the same—with a first-mover advantage—in the Metaverse. The goal is straightforward for the creatives participating in this Metaverse revolution.

We want to make the revenue pie larger in music, film, and other entertainment.

We want to empower artists to negotiate better terms directly with platforms like Apple Music or their existing production agreements.

We want to help create unforgettable consumer experiences that reward users for their loyalty. Therefore, we have built a specific road map that will democratize and decentralize the Metaverse and put control in the hands of the pioneers today.

Metasites will transform the face of the internet forever, establishing a personalized touch and feel that encapsulate the values and potential of users and their brands.

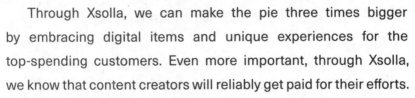

METASITES WILL TRANSFORM THE FACE OF THE INTERNET FOREVER, ESTABLISHING A PERSONALIZED TOUCH AND FEEL THAT ENCAPSULATE THE VALUES AND POTENTIAL OF USERS AND THEIR BRANDS.

Through Xsolla, we can make the pie three times bigger by embracing digital items and unique experiences for the top-spending customers. Even more important, through Xsolla, we know that content creators will reliably get paid for their efforts.

By embracing the blockchain and actively engaging their superusers, content creators will have greater transparency of user transactions, ensuring they know the right amount of money they should receive.

The Metaverse will also streamline payments and ensure the accuracy of creators' royalties. That ensures the traditional platforms cannot take more of the expanding pie, while at the same time, artists will receive a more significant revenue share for their work.

If you still need to catch up on the first revolution of the internet, do not fret.

You shouldn't be concerned if you didn't get a chance to experience the early rise of e-commerce or mobile internet. The Metaverse—and the rise of Web 3.0—will transform businesses and consumers, creating incredible financial windfalls for early adopters and allowing anyone to plant their flag in a transformative and booming digital economy. As we enter the early innings of the Metaverse, I anticipate ample opportunities to discuss the coming shifts in public policy, technologies, and the global e-commerce ecosystem of this new world.

This is my invitation for you to learn more about your potential and how you can build your presence in the Metaverse today.

ACKNOWLEDGMENTS

After I graduated from Harvard, I joined YPO, Vistage, UCLA CEO Forum, and ABL, but my Tiger 21 became my favorite community, and it deeply impacted and shaped my views. Group forced me to write my story as a part of a portfolio defense exercise, and it became the second chapter for this book. And that is how my writer journey begins. Tiger 21 organized a learning event when I bought a sales pitch from my future agent and publisher Justin Batt, who said, "When you are an author you have authority."

I want to acknowledge the entire LA03 Group who become my true friends and mentors: Nicole Diaz, Renee LaBran, Victoria Flores, Armen Yemenidjian, Bill Dorfman, Darren Kavinoky, Eric Manlunas, Jay Schulman, Mark Scher, Mike Jones, Mike Sheldon, Nathan Johnson, Nathaniel Redleaf, Reza Zamani, Rob Dyrdek, Robin Nourmand, Roger Lienhard, Sep Dardashti.

I created a multibillion-dollar enterprise, Xsolla, from nothing. But personally, it's much more important who I became by building it. I want to acknowledge the team who built me and Xsolla: Anton Zelenin, Olga Kovinova, Sam Gaglani, Dmitry Bourkovsky, Berkley Egenes, Menshi, Jingbo, Jayden, Chris Hewish, Sophia

Lisaius, Andrey Podshibyakin, Valentina Sevodina, Aleksey Treshilov, Anton Jvakin, Konstantin Golubisky, Elena Sakova, Justin Berenbaum, Elena Popova, Aleksandr Tokarev, Nick Bondarenko, Natalia Voziyan. Please forgive me if I forgot someone. Everyone in Xsolla is important to me, and everyone is playing their vital role by making meaningful contributions.

I visit a lot of conferences and pick up a lot of ideas from my acquaintances. Sorry, I don't remember your names, only faces, but you shape my views on the business. Here is a list of events I found very energizing and inspiring: GDC, Gamescom, Dice, G-Star, ChinaJoy, E3, Milken Institute, abondance360.

Mike Milken became an inspirational figure for me as the man who found the way to make money by helping other people to make money, surrounding himself with an amazing community and having a healthy relationship with his own health and health system.

Peter Diamandis is North Star Navigator, a source of optimism and massive transformative purpose for me.

Mike and Peter are both local guys, but I would follow them and their events (Abundance, Xprize, Milken Institute summits, etc.) all over the world.

Executive education definitely changed my intuition and world view. I want to thank the faculty of Harvard Business School and the class of OPM 55. I also want to thank UCLA Anderson School, Stanford, Wharton, and Tsinghua University.

I also want to say *hi* to Perm Liceum #2 math class and my dear friend and desk mate Alexey Verchik.

Investment bankers are super connectors in the world of business, and I very much appreciate my team of bankers for their introductions, creating opportunities, and exploring opportunities with me. Hemal Thaker and the whole Goldman Sachs team, Michael Metzger and Drake Star, Nick Tuosto from Liontree and Griffin Gaming Partners, (and Peter Levin, I can't forget about you!), Kartik Prabhakara and Affan Butt at Aream & Co, Maz Yafeh from BofA/Merrill—my sincere thanks to you and all my advisors for your invaluable guidance and support.

I want to thank Xsolla customers who were and are sometimes tough but are always fair teachers for me: Valve, Nexters, Warner Bros., Nexon, Roblox, Epic Games, Ubisoft, and many, many more.

I want to express my appreciation for my two brothers from another mother, Oleksi Savchenko and Kyrylo Tokarev, as well as the 80.lv team who are way cooler than me.

I want to thank my book team for carrying me forward with this once improbable project: Michael Levin, Jesse Aylen, Jennifer Gingerich, Jill Smith, and Kateryna Yermolaeva, as well as my publisher, Worth, and distributor, Simon & Shuster. Also, my special thanks to Ty Lifeset, whose team designed the cover and created a visual language for this book.

Gabe Newel and Valve team are living legends of the industry.

Unity and Epic Games for democratizing game development.

My crypto influencers are Vitalik Buterin and Charles Hokinson. I read a lot of their stuff, which inspired me to write. Dmitry Dolgov, Tim Tello, Rytis, and crypto kid, you are builders! Your time is coming.

I want to thank my family for supporting and comforting me all the way. My daughter who read all my drafts, and my wife who always encouraged me. My two sisters Natalia and Alena, for always being there. And my mom, who I believe loves me but in her very own way.

NOTES

1   "Meta: Mark Zuckerberg Announces Facebook's New Name," Guardian News, YouTube video, October 28, 2021, https://www.youtube.com/watch?v=Sy a_ET05N7E.

2   Citi GPS: Global Perspectives & Solution, *Metaverse and Money: Decrypting the Future,* March 2022, https://ir.citi.com/gps/x5%2BFQJT3BoHXVu9MsqVRoMdiws-3RhL4yhF6Fr8us8oHaOe1W9smOy1%2B8aaAgT3SPuQVtwC5B2%2Fc%3D.

3   Robert Knight, "Metaverse Economy Could Value up to $30 Trillion Within Next Decade," BeInCrypto, November 12, 2021, https://beincrypto.com/metaverse-economy-could-value-30-trillion-in-a-decade/.

4   Casey Newton, "Mark in the Metaverse," The Verge, July 22, 2021, https://www.theverge.com/22588022/mark-zuckerberg-facebook-ceo-metaverse-interview.

5   Salvador Rodriguez, "Mark Zuckerberg Just Brought His Trusted Fix-It-Man to the Forefront at Facebook," CNBC, September 23, 2021, https://www.cnbc.com/2021/09/23/what-mark-zuckerberg-gets-with-new-cto-andrew-boz-bosworth.html.

6   Prasid Banerjee, "Meta Change: From Facebook First to Metaverse First, Says Zuckerberg," Mint, October 29, 2021, https://www.livemint.com/technology/tech-news/meta-change-from-facebook-first-to-metaverse-first-says-zuckerberg-11635446450286.html.

7   Mark Zuckerberg, "Founder's Letter, 2021," Meta, October 28, 2021, https://about.fb.com/news/2021/10/founders-letter/.

8   Huileng Tan, "Facebook Says It Expects Its Investment in the Metaverse to Reduce Its Profits by 'Approximately $10 Billion' This Year," *Business Insider*, October 25, 2021, https://www.businessinsider.com/facebook-metaverse-investment-reduce-profits-by-10-billion-2021-10.

9   "E102: Elon Closes Twitter Deal, $META Uncertainty, Zuck's Historic Bet,
    Big Tech Decline & More," *All-In* podcast, YouTube video, October 29, 2022,
    https://www.youtube.com/watch?v=A-blpJdaCnM.

10 "E102: Elon Closes Twitter Deal."

11 Ryan Mac, Sheera Frenkel, and Kevin Roose, "Skepticism, Confusion, Frustration:
    Inside Mark Zuckerberg's Metaverse Struggles," *New York Times*, October 9, 2022,
    https://www.nytimes.com/2022/10/09/technology/meta
    -zuckerberg-metaverse.html.

12 Ryan Mac, Sheera Frenkel, and Kevin Roose. "Skepticism, Confusion,
    Frustration."

13 As of October 2023.

14 Measured for 2023 at: https://www.nasdaq.com/articles/is-the-worst-over-for
    -meta-platforms-stock#.

15 Mark Zuckerberg, "Mark Zuckerberg's Message to Meta Employees," Meta,
    November 9, 2022, https://about.fb.com/news/2022/11/mark-zuckerberg
    -layoff-message-to-employees/.

16 Jeff Teper, "Microsoft and Meta Partner to Deliver Immersive Experiences for the
    Future of Work and Play," Official Microsoft Blog, October 11, 2022, https://blogs
    .microsoft.com/blog/2022/10/11/microsoft-and-meta-partner-to-deliver
    -immersive-experiences-for-the-future-of-work-and-play/.

17 Jeffrey Goldfarb, "Zuckerberg Motivates Supervoting Stock Resistance,"
    Reuters, October 27, 2022, https://www.reuters.com/breakingviews/zuckerberg
    -motivates-supervoting-stock-resistance-2022-10-27/.

18 Gadjo Sevilla, "Meta Captures 90% of VR Headset Market Share," Insider
    Intelligence, July 6, 2022, https://www.insiderintelligence.com/content/meta
    -captures-90-of-vr-headset-market-share.

19 "Global Social Media Statistics," n.d., DataReportal, https://datareportal.com
    /social-media-users.

20 Harry Baker, "Zuckerberg: Meta Will Continue to Subsidize Headset Cost," UploadVR,
    November 2, 2021, https://uploadvr.com/zuckerberg-meta-headsets-cost/.

21 Casey Newton, "Mark Zuckerberg Is Betting Facebook's Future on the Metaverse,"
    The Verge, July 22, 2021, https://www.theverge.com/22588022
    /mark-zuckerberg-facebook-ceo-metaverse-interview.

22 David Mattin, "A Journey to the Infinite Office," Workplace from Meta, n.d.,
    https://www.workplace.com/metaverse-work-infinite-office.

23 "Remote Work in the Metaverse," Workplace, n.d., https://www.workplace.com
    /metaverse-work-infinite-office.

24 Thomas Germain, "Meta's New Headset Will Track Your Eyes for Targeted Ads,"
    Gizmodo, October 13, 2022, https://gizmodo.com/meta-quest-pro-vr-headset

-track-eyes-ads-facebook-1849654424.

25 Tom Warren, "Microsoft Partners with Meta to Bring Teams, Office, Windows, and Xbox to VR," The Verge, October 11, 2022, https://www.theverge.com/2022/10/11/23397251/meta-microsoft-partnership-quest-teams-office-windows-features-vr.

26 Jay Peters, "Tim Sweeney Wants Epic to Help Build a Metaverse That's Actually Positive," The Verge, December 15, 2022, https://www.theverge.com/2022/12/15/23511494/tim-sweeney-epic-games-metaverses-positive-dystopian.

27 Jay Peters, "Tim Sweeney Wants."

28 Knight, "Metaverse Economy Could Value"; "Citi Report Values Metaverse at $10 Trillion Plus by 2030," Ledger Insights, March 31, 2022, https://www.ledgerinsights.com/citi-report-values-metaverse-at-10-trillion-plus-by-2030/.

29 In 2018, a mysterious explosion killed three people at the gunpower plant. There were multiple reports of explosions again in 2022 during Russia's ongoing munitions production for the Ukraine War. Jennifer Gyuricska, "Three People Killed in Explosion at Gunpowder Factory in Perm, Russia," Dust Safety Science, October 20, 2018, https://dustsafetyscience.com/gas-explosion-perm-russia.

30 "Hotel Rooms 20 Years Ago Were Twice as Large as Some of Today's Offerings," USA Today, November 4, 2015, https://www.usatoday.com/story/travel/roadwarriorvoices/2015/11/04/hotel-rooms-20-years-ago-were-twice-as-large-as-some-of-todays-offerings/83847338/.

31 Maxim Boycko, Andrei Shleifer, and Robert Vishny, "Privatizing Russia," Brookings Papers on Economic Activity, no. 2 (1993), https://scholar.harvard.edu/files/shleifer/files/privatizing_russia.pdf.

32 "05.12.2009: Lame Horse Fire," October 5, 2023, https://timenote.info/en/events/Lame-Horse-fire.

33 "Video Game Market Size, Share & Trends Analysis Report by Device (Console, Mobile, Computer), by Type (Online, Offline), by Region (Asia Pacific, North America, Europe), and Segment Forecasts, 2023–2030," Grand View Research, May 2020, https://www.grandviewresearch.com/industry-analysis/video-game-market.

34 Luke Plunkett, "The Fortnite x Balenciaga Collab Is Everything the Game Deserves," Kotaku, September 20, 2021, https://kotaku.com/the-fortnite-x-balenciaga-collab-is-everything-the-game-1847711963.

35 Knight, "Metaverse Economy Could Value."

36 "CBO Releases New 10-Year Economic Projections," Committee for a Responsible Federal Budget, February 2, 2021, https://www.crfb.org/blogs/cbo-releases-new-10-year-economic-projections.

37 Frank Holmes, "The Metaverse Is a $1 Trillion Revenue Opportunity.
   Here's How to Invest...," *Forbes,* December 20, 2021, https://www.forbes.com
   /sites/greatspeculations/2021/12/20/the-metaverse-is-a-1-trillion-revenue
   -opportunity-heres-how-to-invest/?sh=59ed40984df9.

38 Luke Graham, "Citi Eyes a Trillion-Dollar Industry in Virtual Reality Technology,"
   CNBC, October 14, 2016, https://www.cnbc.com/2016/10/14/citi-eyes-a-trillion
   -dollar-industry-in-virtual-reality-technology.html.

39 Ibid.

40 Elise Dopson, "30+ Influencer Marketing Statistics to Have on Your Radar (2023),"
   Shopify, November 15, 2022, https://www.shopify.com/blog/influencer-marketing
   -statistics.

41 "Global Influencer Market Size 2019," Statista, October 14, 2021,
   https://www.statista.com/statistics/1092819/global-influencer-market-size.

42 "Non-Fungible Token Market Worth $211.72 Billion by 2030," Grand View Research,
   May 2023, https://www.grandviewresearch.com/press-release/global-non
   -fungible-token-market.

43 "Global Web 3.0 Market Size to Reach USD 81.5 Billion in 2030 | Emergen Research,"
   Bloomberg.com, June 1, 2022, https://www.bloomberg.com
   /press-releases/2022-06-01/global-web-3-0-market-size-to-reach-usd-81
   -5-billion-in-2030-emergen-research.

44 Rick Mathews, "US GDP Is 70 Percent Personal Consumption: Inside the Numbers,"
   Mic, September 2012, https://www.mic.com/articles/15097/us-gdp-is
   -70-percent-personal-consumption-inside-the-numbers.

45 Jason Del Rey, "Amazon Ads Are Everywhere. It's Only the Beginning," Vox,
   November 10, 2022, https://www.vox.com/recode/2022/11/10/23450349
   /amazon-advertising-everywhere-prime-sponsored-products.

46 Felix Richter, "From Tape to Tidal: 4 Decades of U.S. Music Sales," Statista, June 24,
   2022, https://www.statista.com/chart/17244/us-music-revenue-by-format/.

47 Joshua Friedlander and Matthew Bass, "Year-end 2021 RIAA
   Revenue Statistics," March 2022, https://www.riaa.com/wp-content/
   uploads/2022/03/2021-Year-End-Music-Industry-Revenue-Report.pdf.

48 "Domestic Movie Theatrical Market Summary 1995 to 2023," The Numbers, 2023,
   https://www.the-numbers.com/market/.

49 "Domestic Movie Theatrical Market Summary 1995 to 2023."

50 "Video Games Market Value to Grow to over $200 Billion by 2023, Despite Declining
   Purchase Revenue," Juniper Research, September 8, 2020, https://www.juniperres-
   earch.com/press/video-games-market-value-to-grow-to-over.

51 Simon Read, "Gaming Is Booming and Is Expected to Keep Growing. This Chart
   Tells You All You Need to Know," World Economic Forum, July 28, 2022, https://www.

weforum.org/agenda/2022/07/gaming-pandemic-lockdowns-pwc-growth/.

52 "Newzoo Global Games Market Report 2022 | Free Version," Newzoo, July 26, 2022, https://newzoo.com/insights/trend-reports/newzoo-global-games-market-report-2022-free-version?utm_campaign=GGMR2022&utm_source=press.

53 "Spotify Revenue and Usage Statistics (2023)," Business of Apps, August 2, 2023, https://www.businessofapps.com/data/spotify-statistics.

54 Lisa Eadicicco, "Here's How Apple Reacted to Taylor Swift's Takedown of Apple Music," Insider, August 6, 2015, https://www.businessinsider.com/apple-reaction -to-taylor-swift-blog-post-2015-8.

55 Rohit Shewale, "45 Netflix Statistics in 2023 (Users, Revenue & Trends)," DemandSage, September 2023, https://www.demandsage.com/netflix-subscribers.

56 Patricia Chang, "U.S. Navy Enlists Virtual and Augmented Reality for Cutting-Edge Training and Recruitment," ARPost, October 12, 2018, https://arpost.co/2018/10/12 /us-navy-virtual-augmented-reality-cutting-edge-training-recruitment/.

57 Joni Sweet, "Video Games Could Hold Untapped Potential in Treatment of Mental Illness," Verywell Mind, July 5, 2021, https://www.verywellmind.com/video-games-could-treat-mental-illness-study-shows-5190213.

58 "Video Games Market Value to Grow."

59 "NVIDIA Powers Digital Dashboard in New Tesla Motors Electric Sedan," NVIDIA Newsroom, June 20, 2012, https://nvidianews.nvidia.com/news/nvidia-powers-digi-tal-dashboard-in-new-tesla-motors-electric-sedan-6622770.

60 "NVIDIA Teams with Microsoft to Build Massive Cloud AI Computer," NVIDIA Newsroom, November 16, 2022, https://nvidianews.nvidia.com/news/nvidia -microsoft-accelerate-cloud-enterprise-ai.

61 Geoff Murray and Rory Heilakka, "The Airline Pilot Shortage Will Get Worse," Oliver Wyman, 2022, https://www.oliverwyman.com/our-expertise/insights/2022 /jul/airline-pilot-shortage-will-get-worse.html.

62 Wendy Beckman, "Using Microsoft Flight Simulator in the Classroom to Improve Student Pilot Aeronautical Decision-Making Skills," International Symposium on Aviation Psychology, 2011, https://corescholar.libraries.wright.edu/cgi/viewcontent. cgi?article=1097&context=isap_2011.

63 Mario Alonso Puig, Mercedes Alonso-Prieto, Jordi Miró, Raquel Torres-Luna, Diego Plaza López de Sabando, and Francisco Reinoso-Barbero, "The Association between Pain Relief Using Video Games and an Increase in Vagal Tone in Children with Cancer: Analytic Observational Study with a Quasi-Experimental Pre/Posttest Methodology," *Journal of Medical Internet Research* 22, no. 3 (March 2020): e16013, https://doi.org/10.2196/16013.

64 "Video Gaming May Be Associated with Better Cognitive Performance in Children," National Institutes of Health (NIH), October 24, 2022, https://www.nih.gov

/news-events/news-releases/video-gaming-may-be-associated-better-cognitive
-performance-children.

65 Elizabeth M. Zelinski, and Ricárdo Reyes, "Cognitive Benefits of Computer Games
for Older Adults," *Gerontechnology* 8, no. 4 (2009), https://doi.org/10.4017
/gt.2009.08.04.004.00.

66 "Paul Krugman's Poor Prediction," *Lapham's Quarterly*, n.d., https://www
.laphamsquarterly.org/revolutions/miscellany/paul-krugmans-poor-prediction.

67 "The Art of Forecasting and Futures Planning," *The Next Wave*, no. 4 (2011),
https://media.defense.gov/2020/Oct/23/2002522458/-1/-1/0/TNW-18-4.PDF.

68 Jennifer Latson, "How the American Oil Industry Got Its Start," *Time,* August 27,
2015, https://time.com/4008544/american-oil-well-history/.

69 "The Art of Forecasting and Futures Planning."

70 Eli Amdur, "Bradbury, Wrights, Claude: Obstacles? What Obstacles?," *Forbes,*
November 3, 2022, https://www.forbes.com/sites/eliamdur/2022/11/03/brad-
bury-wrights-claude-obstacles-what-obstacles/?sh=1ffad83757f1.

71 Richard Brody, "Charlie Chaplin's Scandalous Life and Boundless Artistry," *New
Yorker,* September 18, 2015, https://www.newyorker.com/culture/richard-brody
/charlie-chaplins-scandalous-life-and-boundless-artistry.

72 Editor's Choice, "The Greatest Tech Predictions That Missed the Mark," Information
Age, August 8, 2019, https://www.information-age.com/greatest-tech-predictions
-missed-mark-14423/.

73 Clifford Stoll, "Why the Web Won't Be Nirvana," *Newsweek,* February 26, 1995,
https://www.newsweek.com/clifford-stoll-why-web-wont-be-nirvana-185306.

74 Salvador Rodriguez, "Facebook Closes above $1 Trillion Market Cap for the First
Time," CNBC, June 29, 2021, https://www.cnbc.com/2021/06/28/facebook-hits
-trillion-dollar-market-cap-for-first-time.html.

75 "Internet Growth Statistics," Internet World Stats, 2022, https://www.internetworld-
stats.com/emarketing.htm.

76 "Digital 2023 April Global StatShot Report," DataReportal, April 2023,
https://datareportal.com/reports/digital-2023-april-global-statshot.

77 Leah Collins, "'Huge Value and Huge Risk': Why Twitter's Road to 200 Million
Daily Users Hasn't Been Easy," CNBC, August 25, 2022, https://www.cnbc.
com/2022/08/25/heres-why-twitters-road-to-200-million-daily-users-hasnt
-been-easy.html.

78 "A Message from Chad and Steve," YouTube, October 9, 2006, https://www.youtube
.com/watch?v=QCVxQ_3Ejkg.

79 Mansoor Iqbal, "YouTube Revenue and Usage Statistics (2022)," Business of Apps,
January 11, 2022, https://www.businessofapps.com/data/youtube-statistics/.

80 Tatiana Walk-Morris, "Gartner: A Quarter of Consumers Will Use the Metaverse Daily

by 2026," Retail Dive, February 10, 2022, https://www.retaildive.com/news/gartner-a-quarter-of-consumers-will-use-the-metaverse-daily-by-2026/618474/.

81 Ed Gresser, "PPI's Trade Fact of the Week: American Families Have Cut Their Bills for Clothes and Shoes by Nearly Two-Thirds in 50 Years," Progressive Policy Institute, January 4, 2023, https://www.progressivepolicy.org/blogs/ppis-trade-fact-of-the-week-american-families-have-cut-their-bills-for-clothes-and-shoes-by-nearly-two-thirds-in-50-years/.

82 "Crate and Barrel Appoints Sebastian Brauer as SVP of the Metaverse," Retail Bum, May 13, 2022, https://retailbum.com/2022/metaverse/crate-and-barrel-appoints-sebastian-brauer-as-svp-of-the-metaverse.

83 James Royal, "Bitcoin's Price History: 2009 to 2023," Bankrate, June 14, 2023, https://www.bankrate.com/investing/bitcoin-price-history.

84 "Crypto Wallet Market Size, Share, & Trends Report by Wallet Type (Hot Wallet, Cold Wallet), by Operating System (Android, iOS, Others), by Application, by End-Use (Individual, Commercial), by Region, and Segment Forecasts, 2023–2030," Grand View Research, https://www.grandviewresearch.com/industry-analysis/crypto-wallet-market-report.

85 Robert McMillan, "The Inside Story of Mt. Gox, Bitcoin's $460 Million Disaster," Wired, March 3, 2014, https://www.wired.com/2014/03/bitcoin-exchange/.

86 Nathan Reiff, "The Collapse of FTX: What Went Wrong with the Crypto Exchange?" Investopedia, February 2023, https://www.investopedia.com/what-went-wrong-with-ftx-6828447.

87 "Loyalty Management Market Size, Share, and COVID-19 Impact Analysis, by Development (On-Premise and Cloud), by Enterprise Type (Large Enterprises and Small & Medium Enterprises), and by End Use (BFSI, IT and Telecommunications, Transportation, Retail, Hospitality, Manufacturing, Media & Entertainment, and Others), and Regional Forecase, 2023–2030," Fortune Business Insights, https://www.fortunebusinessinsights.com/industry-reports/loyalty-management-market-101166.

88 Lindsey Finch, "Managing the Customer Trust Crisis: New Research Insights," The 360 Blog, September 6, 2018, https://www.salesforce.com/blog/trends-customer-trust-research-transparency-blog/.

89 Lindsey Finch, "Managing the Customer Trust Crisis."

90 "Marriott Bonvoy Logs into the Metaverse with Debut of Travel-Inspired NFTs," Marriott International Newscenter (US), December 4, 2021, https://news.marriott.com/news/2021/12/04/marriott-bonvoy-logs-into-the-metaverse-with-debut-of-travel-inspired-nfts.

91 Kylie Logan, "Snoop Dogg Is Developing a Snoopverse, and Someone Just Bought a Property in His Virtual World for Almost $500,000," Fortune, December 10, 2021,

https://fortune.com/2021/12/09/snoop-dogg-rapper-metaverse-snoopverse.

92 Allied Market Research, "Internet Advertising Market to Reach $1.08 Trillion, Globally, by 2027 at 17.2% CAGR: Allied Market Research," PR Newswire, November 25, 2020, https://www.prnewswire.com/news-releases/internet-advertising-market -to-reach-1-08-trillion-globally-by-2027-at-17-2-cagr-allied-market-research -301180403.html.

93 Megan Graham and Jennifer Elias, "How Google's $150 Billion Advertising Business Works," CNBC, May 18, 2021, https://www.cnbc.com/2021/05/18/how-does -google-make-money-advertising-business-breakdown-.html.

94 "How Does Google Make Its Money: The 20 Most Expensive Keywords in Google Ads," WordStream, 2011, https://www.wordstream.com/articles/most-expensive -keywords.

95 Mike Schrobo, "The Most Expensive Keywords for 2022," PPC Hero, March 7, 2022, https://www.ppchero.com/the-most-expensive-keywords-for-2022/.

96 Juan Carlos Perez, "Update: Google to Settle Click-Fraud Lawsuit for $90M," Computerworld, March 9, 2006, https://www.computerworld.com/article/2562406 /update--google-to-settle-click-fraud-lawsuit-for--90m.html.

97 "Google Revenue: Annual, Quarterly, and Historic - Zippia," July 21, 2023, https://www.zippia.com/google-careers-24972/revenue.

98 Ben Lovejoy, "VR Apps: Developers Compare Meta to Apple, Accuse It of Hypocrisy," 9to5Mac, June 29, 2022, https://9to5mac.com/2022/06/29/vr-apps/.

99 "Meta CEO Mark Zuckerberg Offers Support to Developers to Bypass Apple's 30% Fees," InfotechLead, November 4, 2021, https://infotechlead.com/digital/meta- ceo-mark-zuckerberg-offers-support-to-developers-to-bypass-apples -30-fees-69558.

100 Peter Murray, "How Faster Amazon Seller Payments Drive Holiday Growth," eComEngine, December 8, 2022, https://www.ecomengine.com/blog/ amazon-seller-payments.

101 "Study Finds Average Cost of Data Breaches Reaches All-Time High in 2022," Morgan Lewis, January 4, 2023, https://www.morganlewis.com/blogs/sourcingat morganlewis/2023/01/study-finds-average-cost-of-data-breaches-reaches-all -time-high-in-2022.

102 Emily Heaslip, "What Small Businesses Need to Know About Ransomware," US Chamber of Commerce, January 23, 2023, https://www.uschamber.com/co /run/technology/small-businesses-ransomware.

103 HealthDay, "Ransomware Attacks on U.S. Hospitals Have Doubled Since 2016," U.S. News & World Report, January 4, 2023, https://www.usnews.com/news /health-news/articles/2023-01-04/ransomware-attacks-on-u-s-hospitals-have -doubled-since-2016.

104 "How to Stop Data Brokers from Selling Your Personal Data," Kaspersky, n.d., https://www.kaspersky.com/resource-center/preemptive-safety/how-to-stop -data-brokers-from-selling-your-personal-information.

105 "Examining Legislative Proposals to Protect Consumer Data Privacy," U.S. Senate Committee on Commerce, Science, & Transportation, December 4, 2019, https://www.commerce.senate.gov/2019/12/examining-legislative -proposals-to-protect-consumer-data-privacy.

106 Emily Crane, "Senate Panel Warned China Has Enough Data for Dossiers on All Americans," *New York Post,* August 9, 2021, https://nypost.com/2021/08/09/ senate-panel-warned-china-has-enough-data-for-dossiers-on-all-americans/.

107 Rachel Treisman, "The FBI Alleges TikTok Poses National Security Concerns," NPR, November 17, 2022, https://www.npr.org/2022/11/17/1137155540/fbi-tiktok -national-security-concerns-china.

108 Charles Arthur, "Google to Pay Record $22.5m Fine to FTC over Safari Tracking," *The Guardian,* August 9, 2012, https://www.theguardian.com/technology/2012 /aug/09/google-record-fine-ftc-safari.

109 "FTC Imposes $5 Billion Penalty and Sweeping New Privacy Restrictions on Facebook," Federal Trade Commission, July 24, 2019, https://www.ftc.gov /news-events/news/press-releases/2019/07/ftc-imposes-5-billion-penalty -sweeping-new-privacy-restrictions-facebook.

110 Reuters Staff, "EU Fines Facebook 110 Million Euros over WhatsApp Deal," Reuters, May 18, 2017, https://www.reuters.com/article/us-eu-faceboo k-antitrust-idUSKCN18E0LA.

111 "The Value of Getting Personalization Right—or Wrong—Is Multiplying," McKinsey & Company, November 12, 2021, https://www.mckinsey.com/capabilities /growth-marketing-and-sales/our-insights/the-value-of-getting-personalization -right-or-wrong-is-multiplying.

112 "The Value of Getting Personalization Right—or Wrong—Is Multiplying," McKinsey & Company, November 12, 2021, https://www.mckinsey.com/capabilities /growth-marketing-and-sales/our-insights/the-value-of-getting-personalization -right-or-wrong-is-multiplying.

113 Amy Gallo, "The Value of Keeping the Right Customers," *Harvard Business Review,* October 29, 2014, https://hbr.org/2014/10/the-value-of-keeping-the-right -customers.

114 Jeffrey Grabow, "Q4 2022 Venture Capital Investment Trends," Ernst & Young, January 30, 2023, https://www.ey.com/en_us/growth/venture-capital/q4-2022 -venture-capital-investment-trends.

115 "Venture Capital Investment Market Share and Size 2022–2027," IMARC Group, n.d., https://www.imarcgroup.com/venture-capital-investment-market.

116 Adam Hayes, "Accredited Investor Defined: Understand the Requirements," Investopedia, July 4, 2023, https://www.investopedia.com/terms/a/accredited investor.asp.

117 "There Are Only Two Plots: (1) a Person Goes on a Journey (2) a Stranger Comes to Town – Quote Investigator®," accessed February 20, 2023, https://quoteinvest igator.com/2015/05/06/two-plots/.

118 Cliff Saran, "Stanford University Finds That AI Is Outpacing Moore's Law," ComputerWeekly.Com, December 12, 2019, https://www.computerweekly.com /news/252475371/Stanford-University-finds-that-AI-is-outpacing-Moores-Law.

119 Knight, "Metaverse Economy Could Value."